<u>Easy Grammar® Grade 6</u>
<u>Student Workbook</u>

Wanda C. Phillips, Ed.D.

PUBLISHED BY EASY GRAMMAR SYSTEMS INC.

7717 E. Greenway Road

Scottsdale, AZ 85260

www.easygrammar.com

© 2006

Printed in the United States of America

PREPOSITIONS:

about	during	toward
above	except	under
across	for	underneath
after	from	until
against	in	up
along	inside	upon
amid	into	with
among	like	within
around	near	without
at	of	
atop	off	
before	on	
behind	onto	
below	out	
beneath	outside	
beside	over	
between	past	
beyond	regarding	
but (meaning except)	since	
by	through	
concerning	throughout	
down	to	

		FREE		

2

Directions: Cross out any prepositional phrase(s). Underline the subject once and the verb twice.

   Example: Kimi lives in the desert.

1. I cleaned for an hour.

2. His father sings in the shower.

3. We walked along a trail.

4. My friend lives near our church.

5. A clerk stood beside a counter.

6. Mimi ran down the road.

7. Seth went to the store.

8. Your book is under the sofa.

9. Everyone except Nikki left.

10. Her brush fell between the seats.

11. A stranger walked toward the policeman.

12. Grandma sits on her patio.

13. Alana lives with her aunt.

14. A dog leaped off the porch.

15. This story is about frogs.

Name_____

Date_____

Directions: Cross out any prepositional phrase(s). Underline the subject once
             and the verb twice.

             Example: His <u>keys</u> <u><u>are</u></u> ~~on the table~~.

1. <u>Jason</u> <u><u>hid</u></u> ~~behind a bush~~.

2. The <u>teenager</u> <u><u>charged</u></u> ~~out the door~~.

3. His <u>bus</u> <u><u>arrives</u></u> ~~before lunch~~.

4. ~~During recess~~, her <u>teacher</u> <u><u>works</u></u>.

5. A <u>picture</u> <u><u>hangs</u></u> ~~above a small window~~.

6. Their <u>dog</u> <u><u>ran</u></u> ~~outside their gate~~.

7. <u>Mr. Jones</u> <u><u>leaned</u></u> ~~against a wall~~.

8. That <u>cat</u> <u><u>jumps</u></u> ~~over the other animals~~.

9. Some <u>children</u> <u><u>raced</u></u> ~~up the hill~~.

10. <u>Mary</u> <u><u>left</u></u> ~~without her books~~.

11. A <u>boat</u> <u><u>sailed</u></u> ~~across the wide lake~~.

12. The <u>boys</u> <u><u>flopped</u></u> ~~into the water~~.

13. My <u>mom</u> <u><u>cleans</u></u> ~~throughout the day~~.

14. The picnic <u>table</u> <u><u>is</u></u> ~~beyond those trees~~.

15. <u>Mrs. Smith</u> <u><u>stepped</u></u> ~~into the bus~~.

8

TEACHING COMPOUNDS

Compound means more than one.

A. **COMPOUND OBJECT OF THE PREPOSITION**:   A prepositional phrase may end with two or more objects.   When a prepositional phrase ends with a noun or pronoun followed by **and** or **or**, check if another noun or pronoun follows it.

Example: They went with their mom **and** dad.

They went ~~with their mom and dad~~.

🍓🍓

B. **COMPOUND SUBJECT**:   There may be a compound subject in a sentence. This means there are two or more subjects.

Example: During the game, Tom and his brother cheered.

~~During the game~~, <u>Tom</u> and his <u>brother</u> <u>cheered</u>.

🍓🍓

C. **COMPOUND VERB**:   Sometimes, there are two or more verbs in a sentence.

Example: <u>Barry</u> <u>caught</u> the ball and <u>threw</u> it ~~to second base~~.

Directions: Cross out any prepositional phrase(s). Underline the subject once
and the verb/verb phrase twice. <u>Starred sentences contain helping verb(s)</u>.

REMEMBER: A prepositional phrase may have more than one object.

Example: I <u>sat</u> ~~on the floor~~ ~~between the **couch** and the **television**~~.

1.   This postcard is from my aunt and uncle.

2.   The speaker talked about cars and trucks.

3.   Joy traveled with her grandmother and grandfather.

4.   We had chicken for lunch and dinner.

5.   *During fall and winter, his family will go to Boston.

6.   This dessert of apples and ice cream is great.

7.   Jack gave his pens to Tim and me.

8.   Sandy ran the race without her shoes and socks.

9.   His friend lives near Carl or me.

10.   Everyone except Mr. Horn and Mr. Smith won a prize.

11.   The children decided to stay by the swings and slide.

12.   *I am going to a wedding on Saturday or Sunday.

13.   *Your wallet is lying under those papers and magazines.

14.   We walked around the fence and the goal posts.

15.   *You may not go outside the square or this line.

Name_____

Date_____

Directions: Cross out any prepositional phrase(s). Underline the subject once
             and the verb/verb phrase twice. <u>Starred sentences contain helping verb(s)</u>.

Example: Both <u>Jessica</u> and her <u>mother</u> <u>went</u> ~~to the store~~.

1. Dr. Stanson and his nurse talked with the patient.

2. *Your towel and sunglasses are lying on the patio table.

3. Mrs. Shane and her daughter walked along the pond.

4. Around six o'clock, the clerk and manager count the money.

5. Gary and I crawled underneath the table.

6. *Melissa or her brother will sit beside me.

7. *Grandma and her friend are looking through the old albums.

8. *Have the swimmers and their parents arrived at the pool?

9. *Before the show, popcorn and candy were purchased.

10. *Marty, Zak, and Patty were sitting behind the team.

11. The fireman and the ambulance driver talked for a few minutes.

12. *Neither Ted nor his sister can come until noon.

13. Toward the end of the day, his friend and he played cards.

14. *The mayor and his wife will not attend the meeting regarding his election.

15. *Outside the back door, a planter of flowers and a tree had been placed.

Name_____

Date_____

Directions: Cross out any prepositional phrase(s). Underline the subject once and the verb/verb phrase twice. Starred sentences contain helping verb(s).

Example: The garbage <u>man</u> <u><u>lifted</u></u> the can ~~into the truck~~ and <u><u>dumped</u></u> it.

1. Vicky sneezed during the assembly and laughed softly.

2. His dog jumps against their door and puts scratches in the wood.

3. A trucker stepped outside his truck and looked at his tires.

4. Mr. Kunes spoke about smoking and showed a slide concerning good health.

5. Everyone except two players ran onto the field and began to practice.

6. We went down several steps and looked into a darkened room.

7. *This bus travels across town but does not stop by the train station.

8. During the spring of each year, her family digs the soil and plants a garden.

9. Each student but Candy sang and played an instrument.

10. The chef cooks throughout the day and enjoys foods like Cajun shrimp.

11. The little girl found a spider below the sink and yelled for her mother.

12. *May Jake talk to you now or see you after dinner?

13. *Miss Franklin will read a story to the children and present a puppet show.

14. Those hikers sat beneath a tree and rested from their long trip up the mountain.

15. Joe raced beyond the fence, jumped over a box, and stood near a parked car.

IMPERATIVE SENTENCES

In an imperative sentence, the subject is (<u>you</u>).

    A. An imperative sentence gives a command.

    B. (<u>You</u>) is termed "**You understood**".

EXAMPLES:

        A. Stay here.

        (<u>You</u>) <u>Stay</u> here.

        B. Please look at the camera.

        (<u>You</u>) Please <u>look</u> ~~at the camera~~.

        C. Hang the calendar on the wall.

        (<u>You</u>) <u>Hang</u> the calendar* ~~on the wall~~.

*Do not underline <u>calendar</u> as the subject.

    1. This is an imperative sentence. (<u>You</u>) will be the subject.

    2. The calendar is that which is being hung on the wall.

Directions: Cross out any prepositional phrase(s). Underline the subject once and the verb/verb phrase twice. Starred sentences contain helping verb(s).

Reminder: In an imperative sentence, the subject is (You).

1. Sit behind me.

2. Toss the paper into the trash, please.

3. Brush your teeth before bedtime.

4. Listen to your parents.

5. Put the picture atop the china closet.

6. Read this newsletter concerning vitamins.

7. Open this gift from Doug and Tony.

8. In the morning, send this to your Uncle Bob.

9. Put the puppy inside the carrying cage.

10. Throw the towels like that blue one into the washing machine.

11. Take this with you to read on the bus.

12. *Do not hang the picture above the large lamp.

13. Follow that car and drive over the bridge.

14. Walk toward the back of the bus and sit by me.

15. *Please don't jump over those fallen logs behind the shed.

PREPOSITION OR ADVERB?

A preposition must be part of a prepositional phrase. In other words, it must be followed by a noun or pronoun.

This noun or pronoun is called the object of the preposition. If there is no noun or pronoun following the preposition, the preposition is not crossed out. The word then serves as an **adverb**. Place **ADV.** above the word.

USE THESE STEPS:

1. Cross out any prepositional phrases.

2. Underline the subject once.

3. Underline the verb/verb phrase twice.

4. Then, look for a word that originally was learned as a preposition but does not have a noun or pronoun (object of the preposition).

   EXAMPLES:

   A. Janet went inside with her pets.

                ADV.
   <u>Janet</u> <u>went</u> **inside** ~~with her pets~~.

   B. During their vacation, they camped out in the woods.

                              ADV.
   ~~During their vacation~~, <u>they</u> <u>camped</u> **out** ~~in the woods~~.   21

Directions: Cross out any prepositional phrase(s). Underline the subject once and the verb/verb phrase twice. <u>Starred sentences contain helping verb(s)</u>.

Remember: **A preposition must have an object (noun or pronoun) following it.**

1. The doctor came in within a few minutes.

2. A teacher sat down between two students.

3. We went up into Grandma's attic.

4. Lisa drove past in an old black truck.

5. Nick and I looked over at the coach.

6. *Some bikers had gone across at the intersection.

7. The winner danced around in a circle.

8. *Has the carpenter gone outside for a tool?

9. A player hit a ball out of the ballpark.

10. *She had not seen a llama before.

11. Your lungs are near to your heart.

12. Her partner rushed by in a hurry.

13. Jump off carefully and wait for me at the dock.

14. From within the cave came a cry for help.

15. A driver came along and asked for directions.

Date_____

A. Directions: Cross out any prepositional phrase(s). Underline the subject once and the verb twice.

To + Verb = Infinitive: Do not cross out an infinitive.

Example: The <u>maid</u> <u>wanted</u> (to clean) the room ~~before ten o'clock~~.

1. His sister likes to swing on the monkey bars.

2. Kyle wants to go to a record shop today.

3. Mr. Harmon decided to leave before halftime.

4. During the play, someone pretended to be a duck.

5. The banker hesitated to sign the papers.

6. We like to watch for odd traffic signs.

7. The reception needs to be in the last ballroom.

B. Directions: Cross out any prepositional phrase(s). Underline the subject once and the verb phrase twice.

A verb phrase consists of a helping (auxiliary) verb + a main verb.

Example: No <u>one</u> <u>has seen</u> Laura ~~for an hour~~.

1. A French poodle had run into the street.

2. I shall scrub the floors during the afternoon.

3. Their parents are golfing after breakfast.

4. A forest fire had been fought along a highway.

5. Everything but the pizza must be purchased before the party.

6. A camel was leading a caravan through the desert.

7. Should we have gone without him?   23

C. Cross out any prepositional phrase(s). Underline the subject once and the verb phrase twice.

Not (n't) is never a verb. Do not underline it as part of a verb phrase.

   Example: The acrobat has *not* performed for the audience.

1. These chairs were not painted underneath the trees.

2. The tourist would not look over the edge of the canyon.

3. Everyone except Senator Brill has spoken regarding the incident.

4. That artist cannot finish his painting until next week.

5. Did the electrician lean this board against the wall?

6. The riders may have ridden toward the mountains.

7. Could Lenny have moved the hose into the garage?

D. Cross out any prepositional phrase(s). Underline the subject once and the verb/ verb phrase twice. Starred sentences contain helping verb(s).

   Compound Object: A preposition may have more than one object.

   Example: An oak tree is beside a shed and a corral.

1. *Johnny is sitting between his father and mother.

2. *That bus is going to Baltimore or New York City.

3. *After dinner and dessert, you may play dominoes.

4. *Sheila does not study with Nancy or Karen.

5. Mr. Lower works at a video store in morning and afternoon.

6. During their field trip, they gathered samples of leaves and flowers.

7. Her teacher came to school without her glasses or grade book.

E. Directions: Cross out any prepositional phrase(s). Underline the subject once
                   and the verb/verb phrase twice. <u>Starred sentences contain helping verb(s).</u>

**COMPOUND SUBJECTS: The subject tells <u>who</u> or <u>what</u> the sentence is about.
Sometimes there are two or more subjects in the sentence.   This is called a compound
subject.**

   Example: A <u>boy</u> and his <u>friend</u> <u>played</u> ~~in the woods~~.

1. A mother and her child shopped at a drugstore.

2. Miss Cobb and Mrs. Lunder are in the tennis tournament.

3. Larry and I go to the park every day.

4. *Forests and lakes are located throughout that region.

5. *A lemon or orange is needed for this drink.

6. *After the bridge game, pie, cake, and ice cream were served.

7. During the evening, a deer and her fawn walked through the meadow.

F. Directions: Cross out any prepositional phrase(s). Underline the subject once and
                   the verb/verb phrase twice. <u>Starred sentences contain helping verb(s).</u>

**COMPOUND VERBS: A verb tells <u>what is (was)</u> or <u>what happens (happened)</u>.
Sometimes more than one verb appears in the sentence.   This is called a compound
verb.**

   Example: <u>You</u> <u>must sit</u> and <u>read</u> ~~for a few minutes~~.

1. Pat hit the ball into right field and ran for first base.

2. In the morning, I comb my hair and brush my teeth.

3. Mark's frog jumped onto a rock and croaked.

4. Before the play, the energetic actors learned lines and practiced.

5. *Does the new boy travel by bus and arrive at school early?

6. Mr. London takes his lunch to the office and eats across the street.

7. *Rings and bracelets were cleaned and placed into a special case.   25

G.   Directions: Cross out any prepositional phrase(s). Underline the subject once
       and the verb twice.
   **IMPERATIVE SENTENCES: (YOU) is the subject of an imperative sentence.   Read
   (You) as you understood.**

   Example: (You) Go to bed immediately.

1.   Keep this dollar in your wallet.

2.   Erase this mark from your paper.

3.   Please finish your homework within the next hour.

4.   Sand the wooden duck for a very smooth finish.

5.   After the game, put the chairs into the trunk of the car.

6.   Drill a hole in the coconut and drain the milk into a bowl.

7.   Take this package to the post office, please.

H.   Directions: Cross out any prepositional phrase(s). Underline the subject once
       and the verb twice. Label any adverb-Adv.
   **PREPOSITION VERSUS ADVERB: A preposition must be followed by a noun or
   pronoun called an object of the preposition. If there is not an object of the
   preposition, the word is not a preposition. (It serves as an adverb.)**
                                    Adv.
   Example: They walked out into the rain.

1.   The parade went past at a slow pace.

2.   We sat outside in the sunshine.

3.   Their brother comes over with his friend.

4.   The children remained inside during the snowstorm.

5.   He did not come through with his friends.

6.   A bird flew in and out among the branches.

7.   Come in and sit down, please.

26

Directions: Cross out any prepositional phrase(s). Underline the subject once and
              the verb/verb phrase twice. <u>Starred sentences contain helping verb(s)</u>.

1.   Your tennis racket is behind the green chest.

2.   The lady walked among the paintings at the art gallery.

3.   *They haven't seen him since the prom.

4.   Mr. Limpski enjoys pictures of pheasants in paintings and objects.

5.   All cars but that black dune buggy are at the starting line.

6.   A zoo keeper gave a talk about wolves and coyotes.

7.   *Chicken in orange sauce was served with creamed potatoes.

8.   Give this apple to your teacher.

9.   *Has Grandma bought a gift for Ebony's birthday?

10. The boys and girls like to play basketball until dinner.

11. After three tries, one of the cowboys lassoed a steer.

12. Jana jumped over the hurdles and dashed past her opponent.

13. Please seal the lid with this masking tape and string.

14. *A baton twirler had not competed before the final show.

15. The dog groomer walked outside with the shampooed dog.

Directions: Cross out any prepositional phrase(s). Underline the subject once and
            the verb/verb phrase twice. Starred sentences contain helping verb(s).

1.   *Three toads were hopping among the rocks.

2.   An odor of perfume drifted into the room.

3.   He placed the toy beyond the baby's reach.

4.   A horse pulled a wagon through the field.

5.   This food is for fish and ducks.

6.   A pillow fell off the bed and onto the concrete floor.

7.   His dime slipped down through a crack in the boards.

8.   *I cannot do it without your help.

9.   A bus of screaming cheerleaders drove up to the school.

10.   *A giant bird cage was placed above the toilet in the bathroom.

11.   During the afternoon, pigeons hopped near the dog's dish.

12.   Wash this out and hang it on the line.

13.   In the movie, a wounded man crawled up to a stained glass door.

14.   Jill and her aunt like to travel along the Hudson River.

15.   Come in, but wipe your shoes off on the welcome mat.

Name_____

Date_____

Directions: Cross out prepositional phrases. Underline the subject once and the verb/verb phrase twice. <u>Starred sentences contain helping verb(s)</u>.

1. A baby crawled beneath a coffee table.

2. A family with two children attended church.

3. Throughout the summer, they travel to the shore.

4. I left without my coat or hat.

5. Before the convention, the women met for a quick meeting.

6. *The postman has come by in a mail truck.

7. Everyone except Bruce dashed across the street.

8. Above the doorway, we hung an arrangement of dry flowers.

9. During the game, their team made three goals and won.

10. One of the triplets ran into the doghouse and cried.

11. A garden of brightly colored flowers is along the western sidewalk.

12. Are Tim and Diana moving near Houston?

13. From Paul's knee to his ankle, a rash appeared.

14. The shoppers wait until the sale to buy sheets.

15. Stand here among these chairs for a family picture.

Name_____

Date_____

Directions: Cross out any prepositional phrase(s). Underline the subject once and the verb/verb phrase twice. <u>Starred sentences contain helping verb(s)</u>.

1. The temperature is below zero.

2. *These red pencils were given to us by the librarian.

3. *A globe has been placed atop the metal closet.

4. Mr. Jacob's car collided with a truck and van.

5. *Do not drink soda with your meal.

6. Animals like dogs and cats are often wonderful pets.

7. The movers placed the stereo between the wall and the stairway.

8. The sun peaked from behind the clouds.

9. *Did the butcher cut the meat into small pieces?

10. A swimmer stepped over me and jumped into the water.

11. The choir chose to stand upon risers for their concert.

12. A reporter and photographer ran out into the street during the robbery.

13. Ten bricklayers decided to work from sunrise until noon.

14. A group of teachers met and made plans for a science fair.

15. *Will you please come and sit behind the steering wheel?

DIRECT OBJECTS

Direct objects receive the action of the verb. In order to have a direct object, there must be an "action" verb in the sentence. Once in a while, a prepositional phrase may serve as a direct object. However, it happens so seldom that, once again, you will cross out any prepositional phrases. Most of the time, a direct object will **not** be in a prepositional phrase.

DIRECT OBJECT:

A. The girl slugged the ball.
                         D.O.
The <u>girl</u> <u>slugged</u> the ball.

   Who is the subject? *girl*
   What is the action verb? *slugged*
   What was the object she slugged? *ball*

B. Some children flew kites at a park.
                         D.O.
Some <u>children</u> <u>flew</u> kites ~~at a park~~.

   What is the prepositional phrase? *at a park*
   Who is the subject? *children*
   What is the action verb? *flew*
   What was the object the children flew? *kites*

COMPOUND DIRECT OBJECT:

A sentence may contain a compound direct object. This means that there are two or more direct objects in the sentence.

   A. They put peanut butter and jelly on their sandwiches.

                  D.O.   D.O.
<u>They</u> <u>put</u> peanut butter and jelly ~~on their sandwiches~~.   31

Name_____

Date_____

Directions: Cross out any prepositional phrase(s). Underline the subject once and
the verb/verb phrase twice. Label any direct object-<u>D.O.</u>

D.O.
Example: The <u>cook</u> <u>makes</u> stew <s>for winter holidays</s>.

1. Dad shines his shoes.

2. She painted her fingernails.

3. Lance put batteries in the radio.

4. A fisherman caught a large bass.

5. The catcher threw the ball to second base.

6. His sister sewed a button on a blouse.

7. Ericka draws pictures of pelicans.

8. A crying toddler tossed a yellow toy onto the bed.

9. Mrs. Billings climbs mountains for a hobby.

10. They placed large pink balloons on the ceiling.

11. The florist has not yet sent flowers for their wedding.

12. We made and ate some chocolate cupcakes.

13. Has the plumber fixed the drain in the sink?

14. During the wedding, Susan and her partner danced a polka.

15. Put the garbage in the new trash can.

Date_____

Directions: Cross out any prepositional phrases. Underline the subject once and
the verb/verb phrase twice. Label any direct object-<u>D.O.</u>

D.O.

Example: <u>They</u> <u><u>sent</u></u> a telegram ~~to their aunt and uncle~~.

1. Robb and Anne make their beds in the morning.

2. Dad rubbed oil on the baby's skin.

3. Peter bought a candy bar with nuts.

4. A mother chased her child across the lawn.

5. During vacation, Mom took many pictures of us.

6. The lady pushed the shopping cart through the store.

7. Micah traded baseball cards at the store.

8. Their dog buries bones in their backyard.

9. The artist carved a duck with a special tool.

10. The Smith family gave a party for Tom's graduation.

11.   Mindy does not want a mountain bike .

12. Mr. Stone and his client ate lunch at a Chinese restaurant.

13.   Has that family built a new house in your neighborhood?

14. Throw that purple frisbee across the street immediately.

15. For lunch and dinner, Greg likes chicken without the skin.

Sometimes, there will be more than one direct object in a sentence. This is called a compound object.

                                              D.O.   D.O.

Examples: The <u>carpenter</u> <u>carried</u> his saw, and nail pouch ~~to his ear~~.

                             D.O.   D.O.

                <u>We</u> <u>saw</u> a clown and an acrobat ~~at the circus~~.

Directions: Cross out any prepositional phrase(s). Underline the subject once and the verb/verb phrase twice. Label any direct object(s)-<u>D.O.</u>

1.   I want those marbles and a yo-yo.

2.   The secretary typed a letter and envelope for the chairperson.

3.   A cafeteria worker piled macaroni and a sandwich on my tray.

4.   Dad makes bacon and eggs for breakfast.

5.   I found a wallet and a comb under the sofa cushions.

6.   Several picnickers threw leaves and pebbles into the stream.

7.   In her garden, Thelma Lee planted tomatoes and lettuce.

8.   Sally and Todd baked two pies and a loaf of bread.

9.   The waiter filled a pitcher and two glasses with water.

10.   A catcher wears a mask and a chest pad for protection.

11.   Kerry dropped a dime and a quarter into the plate.

12.   Give this book and that magazine to your mother.

13.   My brother doesn't like spinach, mashed potatoes, or green beans.

14.   Has the director chosen William or his friend to be in the play?

15.   With Mrs. Molby's help, I have made a heart-shaped pillow and a baby's blanket.

VERBS

A. **An infinitive is _to_ plus a verb.**   (***to*** + verb = infinitive)

Examples: to run   to see   to raise   to like   to enjoy
            to jump   to find   to smile   to go   to eat

B. **A verb of a sentence expresses an action or simply states a fact.**

Examples: Martin <u>mows</u> the lawn each week.   (action)

Mrs. Darnell <u>cut</u> the cake into little pieces.   (action)

Jane <u>needs</u> a new notebook.   (fact)

An apple <u>is</u> on the floor.   (fact)

<u>Verbs that state a fact, as in the last example, are called state-of-being verbs if they</u>

<u>are a form of the infinitive _to be_.</u>

C. **The two main types of verbs are action and linking.**   Action verbs do

exactly what the term implies. Action verbs show action. (In order to have a direct

object, the sentence must contain an action verb.)

Linking verbs are difficult. First, they do not show action. They do exactly what

their name says. They link two parts of the sentence. They link the subject with either

a noun or pronoun (called a predicate nominative) or with an adjective (called

a predicate adjective).

35

CONTRACTIONS

To contract means to draw together. In forming a contraction, we draw together two words to make one word.   We do this by dropping a letter or letters and inserting an apostrophe (') where the letter or letters have been left out.

A. Make sure that your apostrophe is slightly curved.

B. The apostrophe must be placed exactly where the letter or letters are missing.

C. Write contractions in broken form so that mistakes are avoided.

    can't   Note the space between <u>n</u> and <u>t</u>. In cursive, do not attach the <u>n</u> and <u>t</u>.

CONTRACTION	= VERB	+	WORD
aren't	are	+	not
can't	can	+	not
couldn't	could	+	not
don't	do	+	not
doesn't	does	+	not
didn't	did	+	not
hasn't	has	+	not
haven't	have	+	not
hadn't	had	+	not
isn't	is	+	not
mightn't	might	+	not
mustn't	must	+	not
shouldn't	should	+	not
wasn't	was	+	not
weren't	were	+	not
won't	will	+	not
wouldn't	would	+	not

CONTRACTION	= WORD	+	VERB
he's	he	+	is
he'd	he	+	would
here's	here	+	is
I'd	I	+	would
I'll	I	+	shall*
I'm	I	+	am
it's	it	+	is
I've	I	+	have
she'd	she	+	would
she's	she	+	is
there's	there	+	is
they'll	they	+	will
they're	they	+	are
what's	what	+	is
where's	where	+	is
who's	who	+	is
you'd	you	+	would
you'll	you	+	will
you're	you	+	are

*or I will

Name_____   **CONTRACTIONS**

Date_____

Directions: Write the contraction.

1. could not - _____

2. you are - _____

3. I will - _____

4. where is - _____

5. is not - _____

6. cannot - _____

7. they will - _____

8. you would - _____

9. must not - _____

10. she is - _____

11. I have - _____

12. does not - _____

13. what is -_____

14. will not - _____

15. I am - _____

16. was not - _____

17. he is - _____

18. have not - _____

19. there is - _____

20. you will - _____

21. did not - _____

22. would not - _____

23. here is - _____

24. are not - _____

25. who is - _____

26. should not - _____

27. do not - _____

28. I would - _____

29. has not - _____

30. they are - _____

Name_____

Date_____

Directions: Write the contraction for the italicized words in the space provided.

Example: _____You'll_____   *You will* be just fine.

1. _____   The customer *was not* happy.

2. _____   The baby *had not* been changed.

3. _____   *She would* rather ski.

4. _____   *It is* nice to meet you.

5. _____   Mr. Coe *might not* be able to go.

6. _____   Peaches *were not* ripe yet.

7. _____   *I am* very confused.

8. _____   Shelly *cannot* find the key to the lock.

9. _____   *He would* be smart to do that.

10. _____   Their cat *does not* go outside.

11. _____   *Here is* the word in the dictionary.

12. _____   Adam and she *have not* found an apartment.

13. _____   During the holiday, *they will* fly home.

14. _____   This swimsuit *is not* on sale.

15. _____   *I shall* finish this chore later.

Name_____ **CONTRACTIONS**

Date_____

Directions: Write the contraction for the italicized words in the space provided.

Example: ___shouldn't___   Zack *should not* play in the street.

1. _____   *I have* an antique doll.

2. _____   *Where is* the bag of chips, Don?

3. _____   The actress *did not* perform well.

4. _____   *What is* the name of your favorite song?

5. _____   I believe that *you will* learn to water ski easily.

6. _____   *I would* prefer to take a sack lunch.

7. _____   Do you know *who is* the President?

8. _____   He *could not* repair the broken lock.

9. _____   *Do not* go outside during the hurricane.

10. _____   Has Larry told you where *they are* going?

11. _____   Mrs. Ball is sure that *you are* right for the job.

12. _____   Those soldiers *are not* training for combat now.

13. _____   I *will not* get my driver's license for a long time.

14. _____   *He is* the best basketball player I know.

15. _____   You *must not* rush through your homework.

HELPING (AUXILIARY) VERBS

These twenty-three helping verbs must be memorized and learned.

LIST OF HELPING VERBS

do	have	may	should	shall	is
does	has	might	would	will	am
did	had	must	could	can	are
					was
					were
					be
					being
					been

VERB PHRASES

A verb may be composed of one word or two or more verbs placed as a group. This group is called a verb phrase. The last word in a verb phrase is called a **main verb**. Other verbs preceding the main verb are called helping (auxiliary) verbs.

VERB PHRASE	=	HELPING VERB(S)	+	MAIN VERB
can play	=	can	+	play
has been taken	=	has been	+	taken
should have left	=	should have	+	left

A verb on the helping verb list may serve both as a single verb or as a helping verb.

      Examples: I **am** here. (verb)
                       I **am** going to a cookout.   (helping verb)

Some verbs on the helping verb list can also serve as the main verb.

      Examples: Joseph had **been** in a play.   (main verb)

                       Her friend has **been** crying. (helping verb)

In a declarative (statement) sentence, the verb phrase is usually together.

      Example: The box had been sent in the mail.

                     had been + sent

In an interrogative (question) sentence, the verb phrase is often split. Look for a helping verb at the beginning of most questions.

      Example: Did Mario push the button?

             Did + push

Date_____

Directions: Cross out any prepositional phrase(s). Underline the subject once and
the verb phrase twice. Write the helping verb in the first column and the
main verb in the second column.

Remember: Verb Phrase =   helping verb(s)   +   main verb
may run   may   run

	HELPING VERB	**MAIN VERB**
1. Chris has gone to the movie.	_____	_____
2. That worker had eaten in a cafe.	_____	_____
3. She had put the dishes by the sink.	_____	_____
4. The bone was broken in two places.	_____	_____
5. These shorts were ironed today.	_____	_____
6. Karla is driving to a friend's home.	_____	_____
7. The bus should arrive soon.	_____	_____
8. This tour might require an hour.	_____	_____
9. Directions for the test were read aloud.	_____	_____
10. The truck was stolen during the night.	_____	_____
11. This bread can rise by the fire.	_____	_____
12. Ellen could not stay with us.	_____	_____
13. Have you taken the casserole from the oven?	_____	_____
14. Bill had never seen Lake Mead.	_____	_____
15. Did one of the boys swim across the pond?	_____	_____

Name_____   **VERB PHRASES**

Date_____

Directions: Cross out any prepositional phrase(s).   Underline the subject once and
the verb phrase twice.   Write the helping verb(s) in the first column and
the main verb in the second column.

Remember: Verb Phrase   =   helping verb(s)   +   main verb
could have sat   could have   sat

	HELPING VERB(S)	**MAIN VERB**
1. They will look for a new home.	_____	_____
2. The train must have left on time.	_____	_____
3. Would you take me to school?	_____	_____
4. The doctor has set her leg.	_____	_____
5. This chair had been repaired.	_____	_____
6. I shall leave without you.	_____	_____
7. Flowers have been arranged in a bouquet.	_____	_____
8. This purse was found in the closet.	_____	_____
9. His niece is leaving on vacation.	_____	_____
10. Has Ned met the new coach?	_____	_____
11. Their mother should have worn more sunblock during the party.	_____	_____
12. Ants were crawling over my foot.	_____	_____
13. May Sue ride with Beth and you?	_____	_____
14. My pizza might be delivered soon.	_____	_____
15. This candle cannot be stored here.	_____	_____

Name_____ **VERB PHRASES**

Date_____

Directions: Cross out any prepositional phrase(s). Underline the subject once and the verb phrase twice. Write the helping verb(s) in the first column and the main verb in the second column.

Remember: **Verb Phrase** = **helping verb** + **main verb**
will be going   will be   going

	HELPING VERB(S)	*MAIN VERB*
1. Women were standing in line.	_____	_____
2. Frank has made pancakes again.	_____	_____
3. Can you open this jar for me?	_____	_____
4. The car had been painted blue.	_____	_____
5. Water has been poured on her hair.	_____	_____
6. The dog's leg may have been injured by the branches.	_____	_____
7. Shall I remove this from the table?	_____	_____
8. Joy would not work in the garden.	_____	_____
9. Trout are biting in the stream today.	_____	_____
10. Two boys have been trying to surf.	_____	_____
11. Keys might be hidden under the planter by the front door.	_____	_____
12. An athlete must practice daily.	_____	_____
13. Is the roofer nailing the last tile?	_____	_____
14. The real estate agent had not located a new home for the family.	_____	_____
15. Shoes should be worn in stores.	_____	_____

44

VERBS

In regular verbs, the past and the past participle are the same.

The past tense is formed by adding <u>ed</u> to the verb.

Infinitive	Present	Past	Past Participle
to kick	kick(s)	kicked	had kicked
to talk	talk(s)	talked	had talked
to clean	clean(s)	cleaned	had cleaned

IRREGULAR VERBS

Irregular verbs do not add _ed_ to the past tense.

Examples: Today I <u>swim</u>.   (present tense)
Yesterday I <u>swam</u>.   (past tense)

Usually, the past tense and the past participle form are not the same.

Examples: Yesterday I <u>ate</u> fried chicken.   (past tense)
The man <u>had eaten</u> three pieces.   (past participle)

<u>Infinitive</u>	<u>Present</u>	<u>Past</u>	<u>Past Participle</u>
to see	see(s)	saw	had seen
to speak	speak(s)	spoke	had spoken
to bring	bring(s)	brought	had brought

IRREGULAR VERBS

progressive *perfect*

Infinitive	Present	Past	Present Participle	Past Participle*
To be	is, am, are	was, were	being	been
To beat	beat(s)	beat	beating	beaten
To begin	begin(s)	began	beginning	begun
To blow	blow(s)	blew	blowing	blown
To break	break(s)	broke	breaking	broken
To bring	bring(s)	brought	bringing	brought
To burst	burst(s)	burst	bursting	burst
To buy	buy(s)	bought	buying	bought
To choose	choose(s)	chose	choosing	chosen
To come	come(s)	came	coming	come
To do	do, does	did	doing	done
To drink	drink(s)	drank	drinking	drunk
To drive	drive(s)	drove	driving	driven
To eat	eat(s)	ate	eating	eaten
To fall	fall(s)	fell	falling	fallen
To fly	fly, flies	flew	flying	flown
To freeze	freeze(s)	froze	freezing	frozen
To give	give(s)	gave	giving	given
To go	go, goes	went	going	gone
To grow	grow(s)	grew	growing	grown
To have	have, has	had	having	had
To hang	hang(s)	hanged, hung	hanging	hanged, hung
To know	know(s)	knew	knowing	known
To lay	lay(s)	laid	laying	laid
To leave	leave(s)	left	leaving	left

*Uses a helping verb such as <u>has</u>, <u>have</u>, or <u>had</u>.

IRREGULAR VERBS

Progressive

perfect

Infinitive	Present	Past	Present Participle	Past Participle*
To lie *no DO*	lie(s)	lay *DO*	lying	lain
To ride	ride(s)	rode	riding	ridden
To ring	ring(s)	rang	ringing	rung
To rise	rises(s)	rose	rising	risen
To run	run(s)	ran	running	run
To see	see(s)	saw	seeing	seen
DO To set	set(s)	set	setting	set
To shake	shake(s)	shook	shaking	shaken
To sing	sing(s)	sang	singing	sung
To sink	sink(s)	sank	sinking	sunk
To sit *no DO*	sit(s)	sat	sitting	sat
To speak	speak(s)	spoke	speaking	spoken
To spring	spring(s)	sprang	springing	sprung
To steal	steal(s)	stole	stealing	stolen
To swim	swim(s)	swam	swimming	swum
To swear	swear(s)	swore	swearing	sworn
To take	take(s)	took	taking	taken
To teach	teach(s)	taught	teaching	taught
To throw	throw(s)	threw	throwing	thrown
To wear	wear(s)	wore	wearing	worn
To write	write(s)	wrote	writing	written

*Uses a helping verb such as <u>has</u>, <u>have</u>, <u>had</u>. These may also use other helping verbs
such as <u>was</u> or <u>were</u>.

48

Directions: Write the past participle form of each verb infinitive.

Remember: A past participle form will have a helping verb.

Example: past participle of *to shake* -   ___had shaken___

1.   past participle of *to begin* - _____

2.   past participle of *to leave* - _____

3.   past participle of *to freeze* - _____

4.   past participle of *to wear* - _____

5.   past participle of *to run* - _____

6.   past participle of *to eat* - _____

7.   past participle of *to swim* - _____

8.   past participle of *to fall* - _____

9.   past participle of *to throw* - _____

10.   past participle of *to drink* - _____

11.   past participle of *to speak* - _____

12.   past participle of *to lie* (rest) - _____

13.   past participle of *to bring* - _____

14.   past participle of *to set* - _____

15.   past participle of *to choose* - _____

Name_____   **IRREGULAR VERBS**

Date_____

Directions: Write the past participle form of each verb infinitive.

Remember: A past participle form will have a helping verb.

Example: past participle of *to sing* - ___had sung___

1.   past participle of *to sit* - _____

2.   past participle of *to grow* - _____

3.   past participle of *to write* - _____

4.   past participle of *to come* - _____

5.   past participle of *to know* - _____

6.   past participle of *to take* - _____

7.   past participle of *to lay* - _____

8.   past participle of *to buy* - _____

9.   past participle of *to teach* - _____

10.   past participle of *to rise* - _____

11.   past participle of *to blow* - _____

12.   past participle of *to go* - _____

13.   past participle of *to be* - _____

14.   past participle of *to hang* - _____

15.   past participle of *to burst* - _____

Name_____

Date_____

Directions: Cross out any prepositional phrase(s). Underline the subject once and the verb phrase twice.

Example: A tennis <u>player</u> <u><u>had</u></u> (<u>fallen</u>, fell) ~~onto the court~~.

1. That toilet has (broke, broken) again.

2. A credit card was (stolen, stole) from his wallet.

3. Joyce had (bought, boughten) her coat on sale.

4. Have you (rode, ridden) your bike?

5. We should have (written, wrote) a note to Mom.

6. The television show might have already (began, begun).

7. Those rugs have been (shaken, shook) for five minutes.

8. The balloon had suddenly (busted, burst) into many small pieces.

9. Victor may have (flew, flown) to his aunt's place today.

10. The lock to the gate had been (sprung, sprang).

11. I have (brung, brought) my sleeping bag with me.

12. That dress was (wore, worn) by a President's wife.

13. The bell has (rung, rang) for the beginning of class.

14. Should Jo Ellen and her friend have (went, gone) without permission?

15. They were (chose, chosen) to ride on the float during the parade.

Name_____   **IRREGULAR VERBS**

Date_____

Directions: Cross out any prepositional phrase(s). Underline the subject once and
the verb phrase twice.

Example: Her <u>arm</u> <u>had been</u> (broke, <u>broken</u>) ~~during the fall~~.

1. The tomato plant has (grew, grown) very large.

2. Marty had (came, come) to the party early.

3. We could have (swam, swum) for another hour.

4. Grandma must have (driven, drove) to church alone.

5. Have you (ate, eaten) all of your peas?

6. The horseshoe had been (threw, thrown) past the stake.

7. You should have (saw, seen) the puzzled look on his face.

8. Witnesses were (sworn, swore) in by a tall lady.

9. My grandfather may have (knew, known) Babe Ruth.

10. He was (beat, beaten) at the game of chess.

11. Peaches were (froze, frozen) in a small container.

12. Have you (drank, drunk) your apple juice?

13. That baby should not be (gave, given) any milk.

14. During the meeting, someone had (spoke, spoken) concerning new accounts.

15. The students are (teached, taught) about good health practices.

Date_____

Directions: Cross our any prepositional phrase(s). Underline the subject once and
verb phrase twice.

Example: These <u>shoes</u> <u>had been</u> (<u>bought</u>, boughten) ~~in the wrong size~~.

1.   The *U.S.S. Arizona** was (sank, sunk) at Pearl Harbor.

2.   Has the sun (rose, risen) yet?

3.   We could not have (run, ran) another mile.

4.   Doughnuts were (ate, eaten) for breakfast.

5.   Their dog has been (teached, taught) many tricks.

6.   The mail should have (come, came) during the morning.

7.   His brother may have (drank, drunk) the soda.

8.   David's artwork has been (chose, chosen) for a prize.

9.   A strong wind has (blown, blew) all day.

10.   The tourist had never (swum, swam) in the ocean.

11.   Egg whites were (beat, beaten) for five minutes.

12.   Throughout the day, snow cones were (gave, given) to the children.

13.   He may have (did, done) his chores before breakfast.

14.   The stewardess could have (flown, flew) on another flight.

15.   That motorcycle has been (rode, ridden) across the country.

*name of a ship

SIT/SET

To sit means to rest.
To set means to place or put.

FORMS:

Infinitive	Present	Past	Present Participle	Past Participle
to sit	sit(s)	sat	sitting	(had) sat
to set	set(s)	set	setting	(had) set

Two basic items for sit/set:

1. Both *to sit* and *to set* are irregular verbs and must be learned.
2. *Set* requires a direct object.

Examples:

They are (sitting, setting) in the front row.

<u>They are</u> (<u>sitting</u>, setting) ~~in the front row~~.

(There is no direct object in the sentence. Thus, *sitting* is used. In addition, <u>resting</u> can be inserted for *sitting*.)

She had (sit, set) her boots by the bed.
                        D.O.
She had (sit, <u>set</u>) her boots ~~by the bed~~.

Because boots is the direct object, the answer has to be *set*. In addition, <u>put</u> can be inserted for *set*.

Unfortunately, there are times when *to set* will not have a direct object. This usually occurs in passive voice. Hence, give full attention to the meaning of <u>put</u> or <u>place</u>. If <u>place</u> can be inserted for *set*, use a form of *to set*.

54

RISE/RAISE

To rise means to go up without help.
To raise means to lift or go up (with help).

Infinitive	Present	Past	Present Participle	Past Participle
to rise	rise(s)	rose	rising	(had) risen
to raise	raise(s)	raised	raising	(had) raised

Two basic items for rise/raise:

1. *To rise* is an irregular verb; it needs to be learned.
   To raise is a regular verb. Regular verbs add <u>ed</u> to the past and past participle.

2. *To raise* requires a direct object.

Examples:

Smoke was rising from the campfire.

<u>Smoke</u> <u>was rising</u> ~~from the campfire~~.

The player raised the volleyball over his head.
                              D.O.
The <u>player</u> <u>raised</u> the volleyball ~~over his head~~.

LIE/LAY

To lie means to rest.
To lay means to place.

Forms:

Infinitive	Present	Past	Present Participle	Past Participle
to lay	lay(s)	laid*	laying*	(had) laid*
to lie	lie(s)	lay	lying	(had) lain

Lie/Lay is one of the most difficult concepts in the English language. The past tense of *to lie* is the same as the present tense of *to lay*. Remember that *to lie* means <u>to rest</u>.

Two basic items for lie/lay:

1. *To lie/lay* are irregular verbs and **must be mastered**.

2. *Lays*, *laid*, and *laying* will have direct objects.

Examples:

Anna is (lying, laying) in the sun.

<u>Anna</u> <u>is</u> (<u>lying</u>, laying) ~~in the sun~~. There is no direct object. *Laying* requires one. Also, you can insert <u>resting</u> for *lying*.

A doorman (lay, laid) a package on the floor.
                                    D.O.
A <u>doorman</u> (lay, <u>laid</u>) a package ~~on the floor~~. There is a direct object-package. Hence, *laid* is used. Also, <u>placed</u> can be inserted for *laid*.

Name_____   **DIRECT OBJECT REVIEW**

Date_____

Directions: Cross out any prepositional phrase(s). Underline the subject once and
the verb or verb phrase twice. Label any direct object-D.O.

                                      D.O.
          Example: I pushed a button ~~in the elevator.~~

1.   A receptionist answered the telephone.

2.   They built a house by a lake.

3.   The children climbed a tree in the backyard.

4.   Patsy cleans her room every week.

5.   Miss Jacobs sent a message to her company.

6.   He scrubbed the floor with a mop.

7.   Her mother baked a cake for a picnic.

8.   The woman bought a watch for her husband.

9.   Three waiters in black suits served dinner.

10. Throughout the day, the farmer plowed the field.

11. We did not see any lions at the zoo.

12. An expert examined the computer disk carefully.

13. We eat pancakes and eggs for breakfast.

14. Buy this old chair with twisted legs.

15. Have you finished your homework yet?

Directions: Cross out any prepositional phrase(s). Underline the subject once and
the verb or verb phrase twice. Label any direct object-D.O.

                                    D.O.
        Example: He stubbed his toe on a step.

1.   The small child picked a flower for his mother.

2.   The club planted a tree for Arbor Day.

3.   During the afternoon, the boys and girls played basketball.

4.   Is the mailman delivering a package today?

5.   I read an article about the stock market.

6.   Mrs. Betts and Lyle made sugarless jam.

7.   Mom and Dad washed and waxed the car.

8.   That child carries her teddy bear with her everywhere.

9.   Some passengers took a plane from Dallas to Atlanta.

10.   You should have taken your sleeping bag with you.

11.   Did everyone but Todd ride his horse to the outing?

12.   One of the students wrote a letter to a local newspaper.

13.   The maid did not clean the tub or the shower.

14.   Give this screwdriver to your brother, please.

15.   Has anyone seen the blue basket without a handle?

Date_____

Directions: Cross out any prepositional phrase(s). Underline the subject once and
the verb/verb phrase twice. Label any direct object-<u>D.O.</u>

D.O.

Example: The car <u>salesperson</u> <u><u>set</u></u> a sign ~~on the reduced car~~.

Remember: *To set, to lay,* **and** *to raise* **must have a direct object.**
Lays, laid, **and** *laying* **will have a direct object.**

1. A surfer (lay, laid) his board on the sand.

2. My grandfather (sits, sets) by a stream during fishing season.

3. The sun (rises, raises) in the east.

4. Their neighbor (rises, raises) pigs on his farm.

5. Your taco is (lying, laying) on the kitchen table.

6. Harold (sat, set) the table for a week.

7. That lady (lies, lays) by the pool until noon.

8. Bread (rises, raises) in a warm spot.

9. Deanne has (laid, lain) her cards on the table.

10. Jim is (sitting, setting) with his mom and sister.

11. Nick, with a smile, (raised, rose) to his feet.

12. They (lay, laid) on the blanket to watch fireworks.

13. Some spectators had (sat, set) below the bleachers.

14. The policeman (raised, rose) his hand to the traffic.

15. The lady has been (lying, laying) papers all over the clean floor.

Date_____

Directions: Cross out any prepositional phrase(s). Underline the subject once and
             the verb/verb phrase twice. Label any direct object-<u>D.O.</u>

Remember: *To set, to lay,* **and** *to raise* **will have a direct object.**
             Lays, laid, **and** *laying* **will have a direct object.** *Lay* **will**
             have a direct object when its meaning is place.

                                    D.O.
    Example: (<u>You</u>) (Lie, <u>Lay</u>) the clothes ~~on the couch~~.

1.   The boss (rose, raised) his salary.

2.   Jenny is (laying, lying) in the sun without a hat.

3.   That lady always (sits, sets) in the same seat for lunch.

4.   The architect has (lain, laid) the blueprint on the table.

5.   Their grandfather (rises, raises) cattle on his ranch.

6.   A child care worker (lay, laid) the toddler in a crib.

7.   You have (set, sat) quietly for nearly ten minutes.

8.   In the morning, he (rises, raises) the flag.

9.   (Sit, Set) beside me with your books and papers.

10. Grandma (set, sat) her open umbrella near the door.

11. The patient (lies, lays) down after lunch.

12. Mrs. Linnwood is (rising, raising) money in that booth beneath the elm tree.

13. (Lie, Lay) here on the floor to watch television.

14. Has the exhausted traveler (risen, raised)?

15. This can opener has (lain, laid) in the sink all day.

Name_____ **SIT/SET, LIE/LAY, RISE/RAISE**

Date_____

Directions: Cross out any prepositional phrases. Underline the subject once and the verb/verb phrase twice. Label any direct object-D.O.

Example: The <u>sponge</u> <u>has been</u> (<u>lying</u>, laying) ~~on the floor~~ all day.

Remember: *To set, to lay,* and *to raise* **will have a direct object.** *Lays, laid,* **and** *laying* **will have a direct object.** *Lay* **will have a direct object when its meaning is** <u>place</u>.

1. The painter was (sitting, setting) on the curb.

2. A sunbather (lay, laid) on his towel at the beach.

3. Have you (raised, risen) your hand to volunteer?

4. Mr. Markel should have (set, sat) across from me.

5. My friend and I had (lain, laid) the tools beside a bench.

6. Wilma was not (lying, laying) on a lounge chair.

7. Prices are (rising, raising) rapidly on those products.

8. That boy (sits, sets) his dishes in the dishwasher.

9. The entire family (lay, laid) carpeting in a new home.

10. An elderly gentleman (rose, raised) from his chair without his cane.

11. A herd of cows had (laid, lain) in the field for two hours.

12. For her 4-H project, Hannah is (rising, raising) a pig.

13. Throughout the summer day, he had been (sitting, setting) on a porch swing.

14. (Lie, Lay) the bread knife below the counter.

15. That taxi driver (lies, lays) his lunch on the front seat of his taxi.

VERBS

The verb of a sentence expresses an action or simply states a fact.

Examples: The tennis player <u>hit</u> the ball hard.   (action)

                 Barry <u>made</u> a doll for his daughter.   (action)

                 George <u>became</u> a fireman.   (fact)

                 Their bathroom <u>is</u> upstairs.   (fact)

Verbs that simply state a fact are often called **state of being** verbs.

IRREGULAR VERB *TO BE*

You need to **memorize** and **master** the conjugation of *to be*:

<u>**is**</u>, <u>**am**</u>, <u>**are**</u>, <u>**was**</u>, <u>**were**</u>, <u>**be**</u>, <u>**being**</u>, <u>**been**</u>

Present Tense:

Singular: **is**   The bread <u>**is**</u> in the cupboard.

              a m   I <u>**am**</u> hungry.

              <u>**Are**</u> is used with the singular pronoun *you*. You <u>**are**</u> nice.

Plural: **are**   Those children <u>**are**</u> in first grade.

Past Tense:

Singular: **was**   The fork <u>**was**</u> under the chair.

              <u>**Were**</u> is used with the singular pronoun *you*. You <u>**were**</u> right!

Plural: **were**   Several ducks <u>**were**</u> on the pond.

LINKING VERBS

Linking verbs do not show action. They link the subject with a noun or a pronoun, or they link the subject with an adjective (describing word).

noun

Examples: My <u>neighbor</u> <u>is</u> a *cartoonist.*

pronoun

The <u>champion</u> <u>was</u> *I.*

adjective

The <u>referee</u> <u>remained</u> cheerful ~~throughout the game~~.

🍓🍓🍓🍓🍓🍓🍓🍓🍓🍓🍓🍓🍓🍓🍓🍓🍓🍓🍓🍓🍓🍓🍓🍓🍓🍓🍓🍓🍓🍓🍓🍓🍓

To check if a verb (other than *to be*) is serving as a linking verb in a sentence, write a form of *to be* above it. If the sentence makes sense and the meaning is not changed, the verb serves as a linking verb.

is

Examples: The <u>pie</u> <u>tastes</u> good.

was

My <u>friend</u> <u>became</u> a missionary.

There are three easy aspects of linking verbs.

1. Linking verbs never show action.
2. Linking verbs always link the subject with something.
3. Linking verbs appear as a separate list.

The following list of linking verbs must be **memorized** and **learned**:

to feel	to appear	to seem
to taste	to become	to sound
to look	to grow	to stay
to smell	to remain	to be (is, am, are, was, were, be, being, been)

LINKING VERBS: PREDICATE NOMINATIVES

In an interrogative sentence, the predicate nominative may be more difficult to discern. Follow this method. Turn the question into a statement, and invert the statement to prove it.

Example: Is Vic the new vice-president?

                                                    P.N.
                      Vic is the new vice-president.

   Proof: The new vice-president is Vic.

Example: Are you the head cheerleader?

                                          P.N.
                      You are the head cheerleader.

   Proof: The head cheerleader is* you.

*Sometimes, the present forms of *to be* (*is*, *am*, and *are*) must be interchanged when checking for predicate nominatives.

Example: Was the artist the first person to receive the award?

                                                    P.N.
                      The artist was the first person to receive the award.

   Proof: The first person to receive the award was the artist.

Example: Are your best friends Toby and I?

                                                    P.N.   P.N.
                      Your best friends are Toby and I.

   Proof: Toby and I are your best friends.

Name_____

Date_____

Directions: Cross out any prepositional phrase(s). Underline the subject once and the verb/verb phrase twice. Label the predicate nominative-P.N. Then, write the inverted form of the sentence on the line provided.

P.N.
Example: Their <u>sister</u> <u>is</u> the editor ~~of the school newspaper~~.

___The editor is their sister_____

1. Nina was the winner of the race.

    Proof: _____

2. The champion was Jasmin.

    Proof: _____

3. Dr. Post is our dentist.

    Proof: _____

4. Bruno's best friend is Mike.

    Proof: _____

5. Her favorite subject is math.

    Proof: _____

6. Their favorite dessert is a hot fudge sundae.

    Proof: _____

7. Mrs. Moya was her teacher in first grade.

    Proof: _____

8. Their dinner was pepperoni pizza.

    Proof: _____

Directions: Cross out any prepositional phrase(s). Underline the subject once and
the verb/verb phrase twice. Label the predicate nominative-P.N. Then,
write the inverted form of the sentence on the line provided.

P.N.
Example: <u>Mrs. Jackson</u> <u>is</u> the lady ~~in the suit~~.

_____The lady is Mrs. Jackson._____

1.   Barbara's dog is the poodle with yellow bows.

Proof: _____

2.   A Siamese is a pretty cat.

Proof: _____

3.   The best car was that racer.

Proof: _____

4.   Her favorite show had always been <u>Mr. Rogers</u>.

Proof: _____

5.   Burger Haven is the newest restaurant in town.

Proof: _____

6.   The winner of the dog show was a beagle.

Proof: _____

7.   George remained the manager for three years.*

Proof: _____

8.   His uncle became the newest barber at Worth's.*

Proof: _____

*Insert a form of *to be* (<u>was</u>, in this case) to prove a predicate nominative.

LINKING VERBS

Predicate Adjectives:

A predicate adjective is a **describing word** that occurs after the verb and goes back to describe the **subject** of the sentence.

<u>In order for a word to be a predicate adjective, you must have the following</u>:
A.   The sentence must contain a linking verb.
B.   The adjective occurring after the verb must go back and describe the subject of the sentence.

P.A.
Examples: The <u>car is</u> white.   (white car)

P.A.
This <u>bread tastes</u> stale.   (stale bread)

P.A.
A <u>baby feels</u> soft.   (soft baby)

Be sure that the sentence contains a linking verb.

Terry rides a spotted horse.	*Spotted* is not a predicate adjective. The verb <u>rides</u> is not a linking verb*. Therefore, spotted can't possibly be a predicate adjective. In addition, *spotted* describes horse. <u>Terry</u>, the subject, is not *spotted*.

Always use these questions as a check:
1.   **Is there a possible linking verb?**
2.   **Is there a describing word (adjective) after the verb?**
3.   **Does that describing word (adjective) go back to describe the subject?**

COMPOUND PREDICATE ADJECTIVES:
There may be more than one predicate adjective in a sentence.

P.A. P.A.   P.A.
Examples: The Italian <u>flag is</u> red, white, and green.

P.A.   P.A.
<u>Kirby became</u> tired and sleepy ~~in geometry class~~.

*Remember that a help in checking if a verb is linking is to see if a form of <u>to be</u> can be inserted. If this is possible, the verb usually is a linking verb.

was
Example: Otis <u>remained</u> quiet for a long time.   67

Name_____   **LINKING VERBS**

Date_____

Directions: Make your own linking verb quiz.   Scramble the letters of the linking
              verbs and write one per line. Give it to a friend to unscramble.

1. _____

2. _____

3. _____

4. _____

5. _____

6. _____

7. _____

8. _____

9. _____

10. _____

11. _____

12. _____

13. _____

14. _____

15. _____

16. _____

17. _____

18. _____

19. _____

20. _____

Directions: Underline the subject once and the verb or verb phrase twice. Label any predicate adjective-P.A. On the line after the sentence, write the describing word (P.A.) + subject.

                              P.A.
Example: Your <u>teeth</u> <u>are</u> shiny. _____shiny teeth_____

1. The sky is cloudy. _____

2. His ring is gold. _____

3. My pants are dirty. _____

4. The boy was hungry. _____

5. Those clowns are funny. _____

6. A wolf is wild. _____

7. Her nails are pretty. _____

8. His shoes had been scuffed. _____

9. Their bikes are old. _____

10. These beans are stringy. _____

11. The dress is new. _____

12. The bunnies were cute. _____

13. Their answer was dumb. _____

14. His face is red and swollen. _____/_____

15. The secretary was friendly and nice. _____/_____

69

Name_____

Date_____

Directions: This exercise requires several steps; do this page very slowly. Cross out any prepositional phrase(s). Underline the subject once and the verb/ verb phrase twice. Place *is*, *am*, *are*, *was*, or *were* above any linking verb other than a form of *to be*. Label any predicate adjective-P.A. On the line after the sentence, write the describing word (P.A.) + subject.

                                                    is   P.A.
          Example: The <u>man</u> ~~in the blue car~~ <u>sounds</u> angry. _____angry man_____

1. The shell of this egg is brown. _____

2. The banana yogurt tastes good. _____

3. That carved chest feels rough. _____

4. Your steak smells burned. _____

5. The child remained unhappy. _____

6. A hiker grew thirsty in the afternoon. _____

7. Those drivers seem lost. _____

8. The bells sounded loud. _____

9. His hair looks messy in the back. _____

10. The watermelon is too watery. _____

70

SUBJECT VERB AGREEMENT

Present tense means present time.

Plural means more than one.

In present tense: If the subject is plural (more than one), do not add s to the verb.

Examples: Horses gallop through the field.

Those five boys play football.

Sometimes, the subject will be compound (two or more); do not add s if the subjects are joined by *and*.

Examples: Mickey **and** her cousin sing in a church choir.

A frog, a tadpole, **and** a crayfish live in the stream.

In most irregular verbs, do not add s to the verb if the subject is plural.

Example: Some ducks swim on the lake daily.

EXCEPTION: Some irregular verbs completely change form for the present tense.

Example: The women are in a boat on the lake.

If a compound subject (two or more) is joined by *or*, follow these rules:
   A. If the subject closer to the verb is singular, add s to the verb.
   Example: His daughters or **son needs** a ride home.

   B. If the subject closer to the verb is plural, don't add s to the verb.
   Example: His son or **daughters need** a ride home.

Directions: Cross out any prepositional phrase(s). Underline the subject once and
the verb twice.

Example: Carl (stands, stand) ~~by me in the lunch line~~.

1. A guide (lives, live) ~~in those mountains~~.

2. Margo (stays, stay) ~~with her grandmother~~.

3. A snake (crawl, crawls) ~~in their garden~~.

4. The wind (blows, blow) ~~through that canyon~~.

5. That farmer (plant, plants) wheat ~~in his fields~~.

6. A hair stylist (cut, cuts) her hair very short.

7. The librarian (reads, read) ~~to the children on Saturdays~~.

8. The reporter (writes, write) ~~about the burglaries in their town~~.

9. Betty (swim, swims) ~~for exercise~~.

10. A fiddler (play, plays) ~~with that band~~.

11. Our dog (lie, lies) ~~by the front door~~.

12. Her mother (go, goes) ~~to a specialist~~.

13. I (finds, find) many pennies ~~on the floor~~.

14. One ~~of the girls~~ (fly, flies) ~~without her parents~~.

15. Kurt often (wear, wears) shirts ~~with flowers~~.

Directions: Cross out any prepositional phrase(s). Underline the subject once and
the verb twice.

Example: A <u>balloon</u> (<u>flies</u>, fly) ~~into the air~~.

1.   The dog (bark, barks) throughout the night.

2.   This document (is, are) very important.

3.   Linda (drive, drives) a bus for the city.

4.   A tiger (growls, growl) loudly.

5.   My grandfather (golf, golfs) during the spring.

6.   Each of the boys (drink, drinks) water from the large jug.

7.   Aunt Joy (freeze, freezes) corn at the end of summer.

8.   The child (throw, throws) pebbles into the water.

9.   Their dad (build, builds) racers in the garage.

10.   A rattlesnake (strikes, strike) objects near him.

11.   You (is, are) a friend with many talents.

12.   Miss Sanders (jogs, jog) past the old mill.

13.   The jockey (ride, rides) slowly along the muddy track.

14.   He (jumps, jump) off the diving board.

15.   Everyone (is, are) across the street at the carnival.

Directions: Cross out any prepositional phrase(s). Underline the subject once and
the verb twice.

Example: The swans (swim, swims) on a pond.

1.   Those trains (travel, travels) through a tunnel.

2.   Some cooks (make, makes) lasagna without meat.

3.   Many companies (prints, print) materials about smoking.

4.   Several families (lives, live) beyond the city limits.

5.   Saleswomen (talk, talks) to many customers concerning their products.

6.   Their dog and cat (plays, play) together in their backyard.

7.   A few goats (graze, grazes) on the hillside.

8.   The carpenters (work, works) before sunrise during the summer.

9.   My friend and I often (run, runs) around the block.

10.   Trainers (lifts, lift) weights at that gym.

11.   They (bring, brings) their pets to the park with them.

12.   Some volleyball players (hits, hit) the ball into the street.

13.   Some baseball fans (leaves, leave) toward the end of a game.

14.   The relatives at the reunion (sits, sit) underneath a tent.

15.   Your friends and you (do, does) a great job.

Date_____

Directions: Cross out any prepositional phrase(s). Underline the subject once and the verb twice.

Example: <u>Girls</u> (works, <u>work</u>) out ~~in that fitness class~~.

1.   His friends (sit, sits) beside me on the bus.

2.   Gold miners (search, searches) for gold in the Superstition Mountains.

3.   His brothers (goes, go) to Penn State University.

4.   Mrs. Glenn and she (eat, eats) lunch atop a downtown building.

5.   Migrant workers (pick, picks) cherries at those orchards.

6.   Outside the cabin, the children (chases, chase) each other.

7.   Many in the group (do, does) exercises in the morning.

8.   Wild geese (flies, fly) each fall toward the South.

9.   Those swimmers (lies, lie) on floats until sunset.

10.   The furniture movers (push, pushes) boxes across the floor.

11.   Barney, Jenny, and John (likes, like) lemonade with their meal.

12.   The bicycle riders (drink, drinks) water along their way.

13.   At night Christina and I (place, places) our watches between some books.

14.   Over that hill (is, are) several empty houses.

15.   All the men but Sam (appear, appears) in a commercial.

Name_____   **SUBJECT/VERB AGREEMENT**

Date_____

Directions: Cross out any prepositional phrase(s).   Underline the subject once and
             the verb twice.

Example: <u>Lights</u> (<u>shine</u>, shines) ~~after dark~~.

1.   Those turkeys (gobble, gobbles) loudly.

2.   She (loves, love) the dog with the black spots.

3.   Sometimes, I (fall, falls) up the steps.

4.   Many campers (rows, row) across the lake.

5.   Balloons often (burst, bursts) at a party.

6.   We (scramble, scrambles) eggs for breakfast.

7.   He (speaks, speak) English without any accent.

8.   The secretary of that company (types, type) very fast.

9.   Mrs. Lott or Mrs. Campbell (are, is) from Canada.

10.   His broken toy boat (sinks, sink) in the bathtub.

11.   Ned and Deanne (washes, wash) their car before breakfast.

12.   One of the cows (go, goes) into the barn.

13.   That worker (sleep, sleeps) on the grass during each break.

14.   His sister (know, knows) about the meeting concerning the new library.

15.   A mother with a crying child often (leave, leaves) the church service.

Directions: Cross out any prepositional phrase(s).   Underline the subject once
and the verb twice.

Example: A girl ~~in the first seat~~ (play, <u>plays</u>) a clarinet.

1.   The sky (seems, seem) cloudy.

2.   Those twins (dance, dances) at a studio.

3.   I (enjoys, enjoy) all sports but soccer.

4.   The mail delivery (comes, come) in the morning.

5.   Dad and Mom (listen, listens) to an oldies radio station.

6.   That artist (paint, paints) by the ocean.

7.   We often (buy, buys) fried chicken for our picnics.

8.   I (am, is) from the state of Florida.

9.   She (is, am) in a baton twirling contest.

10.   We (is, are) about halfway through this book.

11.   One of the children (do, does) pushups with his brother.

12.   The Hendersons and she (sails, sail) until evening.

13.   This jar of peanuts (cost, costs) a dollar.

14.   Our leaving (depend, depends) on the weather.

15.   The dinners of fried shrimp (taste, tastes) delicious.

VERB TENSES

PRESENT TENSE: **Tense means time. Present tense, of course, signifies present time.** Although present can mean at this moment, it is easier to use "today" as a point of reference for present tense.

PRESENT TENSE NEVER HAS A HELPING VERB (AUXILIARY VERB).

1. Present tense never has a helping verb.

    My <u>mom</u> <u>is going</u> ~~to the mall~~.

    A. This sentence cannot be present tense although it sounds like it. The helping verb *is* makes the verb phrase *is going*.

    B. The verb phrase, *is going*, is actually a separate tense called the progressive tense.

2. To form the present tense, remove *to* from the infinitive:

    A. **If the subject is singular (one), add <u>s</u> to the verb.** (<u>es</u> to some)

        Examples: **to run**: A <u>groundhog</u> <u>runs</u> ~~across the field~~.
        to need: The <u>fireplace</u> <u>needs</u> to be cleaned.

    B. **If the subject is <u>you</u>, <u>I</u>, or is plural (more than one), simply remove the *to* from the infinitive.**

        Examples: **to chew**: His <u>dogs</u> <u>chew</u> ~~on a bone~~.
        I <u>chew</u> my food very slowly.
        You <u>chew</u> gum rapidly.

PAST TENSE: **Past tense indicates that which has happened.**   Although past can mean a second ago, it is easier to use the term, <u>yesterday.</u>

PAST TENSE NEVER HAS A HELPING (AUXILIARY) VERB.

1. Past tense never has a helping verb.

    <u>He</u> <u>has lost</u> his jacket.

    A. *Has* is the helping verb. Past tense does not have a helping verb.
    B. The verb phrase, *has lost*, is actually a separate tense called the perfect tense.

2. To form the past tense:

    A. **To form the past tense of a regular verb, add <u>ed</u> to the verb.**

        to remain: remained   to practice: practiced

    B. **To form the past tense of an irregular verb, change the verb to its appropriate form.**

        to begin: began   to swear: swore

FUTURE TENSE: **Future tense indicates time yet to happen.**
There are two helping verbs that indicate future tense: *shall* and *will*

THE FUTURE TENSE CONTAINS THE HELPING VERBS *WILL* OR *SHALL.*

Note: Although it has become acceptable to use *will* with any subject, use <u>shall</u> with the pronoun *I*. It may also be correctly used with the pronoun *we*.

Examples: <u>I</u> <u>shall answer</u> your question ~~in a minute~~.

The <u>repairman</u> <u>will come</u> by ~~within an hour~~.

<u>Will</u> <u>you</u> please <u>play</u> this game ~~with us~~?   83

Name_____

Date_____

Directions: Cross out any prepositional phrase(s). Underline the subject once and
the verb/verb phrase twice. Write *present, past,* or *future* in the space
provided to indicate tense.

Example: _____future_____   I shall pretend (to be) a monkey ~~in a tree~~.

1. _____   Terry rollerskates to his friend's house.

2. _____   Terry rollerskated with his sister.

3. _____   Tonight, Terry will rollerskate around the park.

1. _____   She drinks juice for breakfast.

2. _____   The lady will drink milk with her meal.

3. _____   She drank bottled water from France.

1. _____   For my speech, I shall talk about crime.

2. _____   I talk with my friends after school.

3. _____   During the weekend, I talked to your sister.

1. _____   The cement truck driver ate his lunch.

2. _____   The cement truck driver eats at a fast food place.

3. _____   The cement truck driver will eat dinner in a few hours.

1. _____   That model will pose in many outfits.

2. _____   The model posed with an umbrella.

3. _____   The model poses for a fashion catalog.

84

Name_____   **VERB TENSES**

Date_____

Directions: Cross out any prepositional phrase(s). Underline the subject once and
the verb/verb phrase twice. Write *present*, *past*, or *future* in the space
provided to indicate verb tense.

Example: _____past_____   <u>She</u> <u>laughed</u> ~~at my joke~~.

1. _____   These girls swim in the ocean.

2. _____   Mom will swim twenty laps.

3. _____   My cousin swam on a high school team.

1. _____   A judge will speak about courtroom conduct.

2. _____   The father spoke to the child about his behavior.

3. _____   The professor speaks three languages.

1. _____   Darla poured honey into her tea.

2. _____   You pour with your left hand.

3. _____   This rain will pour for another hour.

1. _____   Grandpa bakes apples with cinnamon.

2. _____   I shall bake an eggless cake.

3. _____   A loaf of bread baked in the oven.

1. _____   Before lunch, a businesswoman will fly to Chicago.

2. _____   Our bird flies all over the house.

3. _____   Bees flew around the barn.

85

Name_____   **VERB TENSES**

Date_____

Directions: Write the form of the tense on the line.

　　　　　Example: present tense of *to find* - _____find, finds_____

1. past tense of *to decide* -_____

2. present tense of *to choose* - _____

3. future tense of *to turn* - _____

4. past tense of *to take* - _____

5. present tense of *to swing* - _____

6. future tense of *to follow* - _____

7. present tense of *to shop* - _____

8. past tense of *to call* - _____

9. future tense of *to skip* - _____

10. present tense of *to be* - _____

86

Name_____   **VERB TENSES**

Date_____

Directions: Write a **sentence** using the correct verb tense.

Example: present of *to lean* - _____Tom leans on his elbow when thinking._____

1. past of *to lift* - _____

2. future of *to go* - _____

3. present of *to cut* - _____

4. present of *to wash* - _____

5. past of *to cook* - _____

6. past of *to paint* - _____

7. future of *to eat* - _____

8. future of *to visit* - _____

9. past of *to smile* - _____

10. present of *to like* - _____

Name_____   **VERBS**

Date_____

Directions: Cross out any prepositional phrase(s). Underline the subject once and
the verb/verb phrase twice.

Example: <u>Each</u> ~~of the boys and girls~~ <u>enjoys</u> ice cream cones.

1. A policewoman directs traffic on Main Street.

2. Some daisies grow under that tree.

3. We will travel to Minnesota during Christmas vacation.

4. The tree is shedding its leaves.

5. Several steers graze in the meadow.

6. Mickey flies a helicopter for the U.S. Army.

7. We should have waited until the end of the shower.

8. The couple has gone out to dinner.

9. Are you studying for an exam?

10. The lid of the jigsaw puzzle is lying on the coffee table.

11. He has scrubbed and waxed the floor.

12. A teacher and a pupil had been given awards by a women's club.

13. Look out the window at the street sweeper.

14. Will you be leaving during Labor Day weekend in September?

15. One of the paramedics jumped out of the fire truck to help.

Name_____   **VERBS**

Date_____

Directions: Cross out any prepositional phrase(s). Underline the subject once and
the verb/verb phrase twice.

Example: <u>Most</u> ~~of the chickens~~ <u>were sitting</u> ~~in the coop~~.

1. Ted lives near the beach.

2. The pants were ironed yesterday.

3. The vitamins had been sealed for safety.

4. You and I should ride on the rollercoaster.

5. Below the sink is a drawing board.

6. After the game, we will drive to a restaurant.

7. A ping pong ball was pitched up in the air.

8. Sit beneath the patio for a rest.

9. Sarah bought a poster and hung it on her wall.

10. I am not in this photograph of our family gathering.

11. A hummingbird flew in and sat upon a branch.

12. Didn't Mayor Hines ask for a map of Germany?

13. The manager of the team sat inside the dugout during the game.

14. Marilyn, Jana, and she want to stay until midnight.

15. One of the triplets may have been given that ring.

Name_____   **VERBS**

Date_____

Directions: Cross out any prepositional phrase(s). Underline the subject once and the
             verb/verb phrase twice.

   Example: You must take the ice cream ~~from the freezer~~.

   1. The puppets are entertaining the children.

   2. That cute little puppy begs for food.

   3. A dog trainer walked across the lawn with a collie.

   4. A soccer player kicked the ball and made a goal.

   5. Before lunch, the cafeteria worker cleaned his hands with soap and water.

   6. May I see the slides of your trip to Japan?

   7. Clint and Shawna washed the clothes and hung them on the clothesline.

   8. Nobody could have known the combination to the lock.

   9.   An office clerk sorts mail and distributes it among the employees.

  10. I can't bake the cake or decorate it for you.

  11. Open the car door for your brother and sister.

  12. One of the guards must have come into the building early.

  13. Yesterday, the kindergartner would not sit or stand by the teacher.

  14. A mother with her children in a baby carriage strolled through the park.

  15. Martha's mother and dad were invited to the White House by the President.
90

Name_____

Date_____

A. Directions: Write the contraction.

1. I am - _____   6. has not - _____

2. do not - _____   7. I shall - _____

3. we have - _____   8. who is - _____

4. are not - _____   9. will not - _____

5. they are - _____   10. she is - _____

B. Directions: Write the 23 helping (auxiliary) verbs on the following lines.

_____

_____

_____

C. Directions: Cross out any prepositional phrase(s). Underline the subject once and the verb/verb phrase twice. Write the helping verb(s) in the first column and the main verb in the second column.

	HELPING VERB(S)	MAIN VERB
1. I can leave in a minute.	_____	_____
2. That car is going too fast.	_____	_____
3. A light bulb was broken.	_____	_____
4. His tooth had been chipped in the fall.	_____	_____
5. May the usher escort you?	_____	_____
6. We should have arrived earlier.	_____	_____
7. Did a tornado appear near our town?	_____	_____

Date_____

D.   Directions: Cross out any prepositional phrase(s). Underline the subject once
                         and the verb/verb phrase twice. Label any direct object-<u>D.O.</u>

1.   He (sat, set) the carpet cleaner by the couch.

2.   The book is (lying, laying) on the desk.

3.   The sun has (risen, rose).

4.   Some fans had (sat, set) outside the stadium for an hour.

5.   Before lunch, the diver (lies, lays) on the sand with his dog.

6.   Mrs. Sharp and Annie (raised, rose) chickens in their backyard.

7.   She (lay, laid) the blanket across the bed.

E.   Directions: List the linking verbs (12 infinitives + 8).

_____

_____

F.   Directions: Cross out any prepositional phrase(s).   Underline the subject once
                         and the verb/verb phrase twice.   Write <u>A</u> in the space if the verb is
                         action.   Write <u>L</u> in the space if the verb is linking.
**Remember: Write *is, am, are, was*, or *were* above a verb you think is
                      linking.   If the meaning is not changed, the verb is usually
                      linking.**

                                                                      is
          Example: __L__   The hot <u>chocolate</u> <u>smells</u> good.

1.   _____   A pelican scooped a fish from the water.

2.   _____   The chili tastes very spicy.

3.   _____   That mother feels happy about her raise.

4.   _____   An accountant adds numbers.

5.   _____   Krista tasted the beef stew.

6.   _____   A customer with a return item looked angry.

Name_____ **VERB REVIEW**

Date_____

G. Directions: Cross out any prepositional phrase(s). Underline the subject once
and the verb/verb phrase twice. Label any predicate nominative-P.N.
Write the proof on the line provided.

P.N.
Example: Judy <u>became</u> the new bill collector.
Proof: ____The new bill collector is Judy.____

1. Paul is the leader of his club.

Proof: _____

2. His best dive was the jackknife.

Proof: _____

3. Lenny will be the next senator.

Proof: _____

4. His favorite color of the rainbow is red.

Proof: _____

5. Captain John Smith became a leader of Jamestown.

Proof: _____

H. Directions: Cross out any prepositional phrase(s). Underline the subject once
and the verb/verb phrase twice. Label any predicate adjective-P.A.
Write the predicate adjective and the subject on the line to the right.

P.A.
Example: The <u>handle</u> ~~of the wagon~~ <u>is</u> yellow. ____yellow handle____

1. This painting looks old. _____

2. His jeans are black with a red patch. _____

3. Those curtains seem too long. _____

4. This cement feels rough. _____

5. A hurricane can be violent. _____

93

Name_____   **VERB REVIEW**

Date_____

I. Directions: Cross out any prepositional phrase(s). Underline the subject once
                 and the verb twice. Be sure that the subject and verb agree.

   Example: One ~~of the dogs~~ (<u>is</u>, are) a German shepherd.

   1. Wasps (build, builds) mud hives.

   2. Her niece (is, are) in the U.S. Navy.

   3. The boy (carve, carves) whistles.

   4. My brother and I (rinses, rinse) dishes at our house.

   5. One of the roosters (crow, crows) early in the morning.

   6. A lawyer (discusses, discuss) a case with his client.

   7. His sister (sneak, sneaks) around the house.

J. Directions: Cross out any prepositional phrase(s). Underline the subject once and
                 the verb/verb phrase twice. Write the tense: *present*, *past*, or *future*
                 in the space provided.

   1. _____ Your headlight is out.

   2. _____ I shall tell the story to some children.

   3. _____ Maurny called the veterinarian about her sick cat.

   4. _____ A mechanic repairs my car.

   5. _____ Their grandfathers go deep-sea fishing.

   6. _____ A dentist will speak to us concerning brushing.

   7. _____ A branch and a log fell across the road.

94

Name_____   **VERB REVIEW**

Date_____

K.   Directions: Cross out any prepositional phrase(s). Underline the subject once and
      the verb/verb phrase twice.

      Example: A <u>minnow</u> <u>has</u> (swam, <u>swum</u>) ~~into my net~~.

1.   A dish of sherbet was (given, gave) to the elderly lady.

2.   Janice's uncle has (come, came) for a visit.

3.   We must have (taken, took) the wrong road.

4.   A group of Girl Scouts had (rode, ridden) into the forest.

5.   My friend and I have (drank, drunk) the vanilla milkshake.

6.   Should Mr. Lemon have (eaten, ate) five pieces of pizza?

7.   The tennis balls were (brought, brung) onto the courts.

L.   Directions: Cross out any prepositional phrase(s). Underline the subject once
      and the verb/verb phrase twice.

1.   A whiff of roast beef floated through the air.

2.   A meal of mashed potatoes, peas, and fish was served at six o'clock.

3.   Has anyone seen the album of family pictures?

4.   A player cannot be angry with the umpire's call.

5.   A janitor washed the windows and dried them with newspaper.

6.   Hand this statue to the lady in the red striped suit.

7.   A church bulletin had been handed out to all members and guests.

95

Name_____   **CUMULATIVE REVIEW**

Date_____

A.   Directions: List 50 prepositions.

1. _____	14. _____	27. _____	40. _____
2. _____	15. _____	28. _____	41. _____
3. _____	16. _____	29. _____	42. _____
4. _____	17. _____	30. _____	43. _____
5. _____	18. _____	31. _____	44. _____
6. _____	19. _____	32. _____	45. _____
7. _____	20. _____	33. _____	46. _____
8. _____	21. _____	34. _____	47. _____
9. _____	22. _____	35. _____	48. _____
10. _____	23. _____	36. _____	49. _____
11. _____	24. _____	37. _____	50. _____
12. _____	25. _____	38. _____	
13. _____	26. _____	39. _____	

B.   Directions: Cross out any prepositional phrase(s).   Underline the subject once
         and the verb/verb phrase twice.   Label any direct object-<u>D.O.</u>

1.   The boy in the rodeo chased a steer around the corral.

2.   They threw snowballs at their friend.

3.   Mrs. Sands chose a brown carpeting for her office.

4.   Billy sends cards to his grandparents in Chicago.

5.   A small kitten chased a yarn ball across the floor.

96

CONJUNCTIONS

Conjunctions are connecting words.

The most common conjunctions are called coordinating conjunctions; they are: *and, but, or.*

Conjunctions connect prepositions: His dog ran *under* the bed **or** *into* the closet.

Conjunctions connect adjectives (describing words): I like that *blue* **and** *gray* towel.

Conjunctions connect verbs: He *made* **and** *baked* a pie.

Conjunctions connect interjections: *Wow* **and** *hurrah* ! We did it!

Conjunctions connect nouns (words that name people, places, and things):
> *Pizza* **and** *cola* were served.

Conjunctions connect pronouns (words that take the place of nouns):
> *She* **or** *I* will be your partner.

Conjunctions connect adverbs (words that tell how, when, where, to what extent):
> Step on the brake *quickly* **but** *carefully.*

Conjunctions connect phrases (groups of words):
> The man enjoys *seeing the ocean* **and** *wading in it.*

Conjunctions connect sentences: *I like thunder,* **but** *it can be extremely loud.*

Note: <u>But</u> is a preposition, not a conjunction, when it means <u>except</u>.

Name_____   **CONJUNCTIONS**

Date_____

Directions: Circle any conjunction(s).

1. Potatoes, onion, and garlic were placed on the hot coals.

2. You need to take your umbrella or your jacket with you.

3. Her jacket is large but very stylish.

4. Hamburgers or hot dogs were served from the grill.

5. The ship steamed out of the harbor and picked up speed.

6. Mr. and Mrs. Jenkel are coming, but they will be late.

7. Any food items or money for the needy may be given to Harriet and Bobby.

8. His speech was interesting, but it didn't help solve the problem.

9. A flamingo or a heron was by the island's waterlilies.

10. They like to go to Minnesota and Michigan, but New York is their favorite.

11. His aunt or uncle attended Shippensburg University but did not graduate.

12. The house was stuccoed and painted, but it wasn't completed.

13. A horse or a mule leads the team, but it isn't moving fast.

14. In the afternoon, Jason or his sister went to a bakery and a deli.

15. A minister and his assistant met the couple, but they did not have lunch with them.

NOUNS

Nouns name a person, place, or thing.

CONCRETE AND ABSTRACT NOUNS:

Concrete nouns usually can be seen: board, fork, person, coyote, book

> NOTE: Some concrete nouns technically cannot be seen unless examined in very small parts (atoms). Examples: air, breath

Abstract nouns are those that cannot be seen: honesty, love, friendship

To test if a word might be an abstract noun:

A. Check to see if the word describes any other word in the sentence. If it does, STOP. It's a describing word called an adjective.

   Example: This friendship ring is beautiful.

   In this sentence, *friendship* is an adjective that describes ring. Thus, *friendship* is not a noun.

B. If the word does not qualify as an adjective, try placing <u>the</u> in front of it. If you can put <u>the</u> in front of the word, it is usually a noun.

   Example: My friendship with Mickey is very important.

   In this sentence, you can say <u>the</u> *friendship*; therefore, *friendship* is a noun.

Name_____

Date_____

Directions: In the space provided, place <u>C</u> if the noun is concrete and <u>A</u> if the noun is abstract.

1. _____ glass

2. _____ letter

3. _____ love

4. _____ peace

5. _____ fire

6. _____ chain

7. _____ justice

8. _____ toe

9. _____ pony

10. _____ desert

11. _____ laughter

12. _____ squirrel

13. _____ wisdom

14. _____ mouth

15. _____ woods

16. _____ patience

17. _____ lamp

18. _____ freedom

19. _____ loyalty

20. _____ vitamin

21. _____ beauty

22. _____ thongs

23. _____ syrup

24. _____ happiness

25. _____ plug

Name_____

Date_____

Directions: Three nouns in each row are concrete; one noun is abstract. Place the letter of the abstract noun in the space provided.

Example: __D__ (A) barn   (B) apple   (C) lime   (D) dislike

1. _____ (A) watch   (B) hammer   (C) loneliness   (D) disk

2. _____ (A) camera   (B) mercy   (C) ditch   (D) curtain

3. _____ (A) carrot   (B) candle   (C) kindness   (D) pilot

4. _____ (A) pillow   (B) pride   (C) sugar   (D) bullet

5. _____ (A) magazine   (B) air   (C) eagerness   (D) calf

6. _____ (A) spider   (B) enthusiasm (C) bandage   (D) necklace

7. _____ (A) tree   (B) joy   (C) butter   (D) lipstick

8. _____ (A) friendship (B) lantern   (C) heart   (D) needle

9. _____ (A) eyelash   (B) tire   (C) hat   (D) fear

10. _____ (A) window   (B) time   (C) grease   (D) vase

11. _____ (A) shirt   (B) bread   (C) pumpkin   (D) love

12. _____ (A) star   (B) desk   (C) sadness   (D) rug

13. _____ (A) fern   (B) rock   (C) caring   (D) book

14. _____ (A) smoke   (B) comb   (C) tiredness   (D) puddle

15. _____ (A) bag   (B) pen   (C) amazement   (D) ticket

NOUNS

Nouns name persons, places, or things.

Sometimes a word will be a noun in one sentence but be used as a verb in another sentence.

Example: A _steer_ is standing by a watering trough.   (NOUN)

The driver <u>can _steer_</u> in and out through traffic.   (VERB)

In the first sentence, _steer_, an animal, is a noun.
Steer in the second sentence is a verb telling what the driver can do.

Example: We went to a _show_ in the afternoon.   (NOUN)

They <u>_show_</u> home videos to their friends.   (VERB)

In the first sentence, _show_ is a noun, the object of the preposition: ~~to a show~~.
In sentence two, _show_ is a verb telling what they do with home videos.

Sometimes, a word can serve as a noun, a verb, or an adjective.

Example: The _mail_ is lying on the counter.   (NOUN)

<u>Did</u> you <u>_mail_</u> the letters?   (VERB)

Their _mail_ carrier comes before noon.   (ADJECTIVE)

Name_____

Date_____

NOUNS,
Adjectives, or Verbs?

A. Directions: Write <u>N</u> if the underlined word is a noun; write <u>A</u> if the underlined word is an adjective.

1. _____ This <u>hamburger</u> is tasty.

2. _____ My <u>hamburger</u> bun has become soggy.

3. _____ Hand me that <u>tool,</u> please.

4. _____ The <u>tool</u> box is in the shed beside the barn.

5. _____ Her <u>jewelry</u> case has been stolen.

6. _____ The queen's <u>jewelry</u> is very expensive.

7. _____ Your last <u>grocery</u> is a box of cereal.

8. _____ This <u>grocery</u> cart has a broken wheel.

9. _____ Jeanette made a <u>craft</u> at her friend's house.

10. _____ The couples enjoyed the Christmas <u>craft</u> show.

B. Directions: Write <u>N</u> if the underlined word is a noun; write <u>V</u> if the underlined word is a verb.

1. _____ The <u>answer</u> has been written in ink.

2. _____ He didn't <u>answer</u> the first question.

3. _____ Would you <u>push</u> me on this swing?

4. _____ Kimberly gave Karen a <u>push</u> and ran off.

5. _____ These house <u>plants</u> need to be watered.

6. _____ She <u>plants</u> a garden early in the spring.

7. _____ Why did you <u>slip</u> on the floor?

8. _____ Someone handed the auctioneer a <u>slip</u> of paper.

105

Name_____ **NOUNS,**
Adjectives, or Verbs?

Date_____

A.   Directions: Write <u>N</u> if the underlined word is a noun; write <u>A</u> if the underlined word
                       is an adjective.

1. _____   The <u>garage</u> sale had been successful.

2. _____   The two mechanics pushed the car into the <u>garage</u>.

3. _____   Would you like a <u>banana</u> with your cereal?

4. _____   Did you fall on a <u>banana</u> peel?

5. _____   A <u>bear</u> roams through those woods.

6. _____   A <u>bear</u> trap was found by some campers.

7. _____   The nurse laid the baby on his <u>stomach</u>.

8. _____   My <u>stomach</u> ache seems to be getting worse.

B.   Directions: Write <u>N</u> on the line if the underlined word is a noun; write <u>V</u> on the line
                       if the underlined word is a verb.

1. _____   Take this <u>change</u> and put it in the machine.

2. _____   He will <u>change</u> the knobs on the cupboard doors.

3. _____   When the snow ends, we will <u>shovel</u> the sidewalk.

4. _____   The construction worker used a <u>shovel</u> to smooth some dirt.

5. _____   She has a <u>run</u> in her stocking.

6. _____   Their quarterback had <u>run</u> the length of the field.

7. _____   <u>Lift</u> the latch and open the gate, please.

8. _____   That was her first ride on a ski <u>lift</u>.

9. _____   A <u>load</u> of hay was pulled by a large red tractor.

10. _____   Did you <u>load</u> the dishwasher yet?

106

NOUNS

Nouns name persons, places, things, and ideas.

Noun Determiners

Determiners help to identify nouns. Determiners are like RED lights. When you see a determiner, STOP and check to see if a noun follows it. The noun may be the next word or several words after the determiner.

Classification of Determiners:
A. Articles: **a, an, the**
B. Demonstratives: **this, that, those, these**
C. Numbers: examples: **two** pizzas, **fifty** dollars
D. Possessive adjectives (also called possessive pronouns used as adjectives):
   my, his, her, your, its, our, their
E. Possessive nouns (used as adjectives): examples: Barry's van, ladies' club
F. Indefinites: examples: **some, few, many, several, no, any**

A. **A**, **an**, and **the** will come before a noun and occasionally a pronoun. There may be other words between them.
   Examples: **a** city <u>park</u>   **(place)**
   an <u>officer</u>   **(person)**
   the pencil <u>sharpener</u>   **(thing)**

B. The demonstratives are: **this, that, those,** and **these.** Demonstratives may signal for a noun to follow. However, they may stand alone. When **this, that, those,** or **these** does not have a noun following closely, it will not be a determiner.

                              noun
   Examples: **This** door is extremely heavy.
                              noun
               These potato chips are too salty.

               That is funny!

               That is not a determiner; a noun doesn't follow it.
               What is funny? The answer is not given.

C. Numbers may signal a noun. Stop to determine if a person, place, or thing follows a number.

                                         noun

Examples: The mail carrier delivered **two** large envelopes.

                              noun

          The concert ticket costs **twelve** dollars.

          I want **two**!
          Two is not a determiner here. Two what? The answer isn't given.

D. Possessive pronouns used as determiners are: **my**, **his**, **her**, **its**, **your**, **our**, and **their.** These usually signal a noun. Always STOP and check if a noun (person, place, or thing) follows it. Remember: Sometimes, other words will separate the possessive pronoun and the noun.

                        noun

Examples: **My** big brother is nice.   (person)

                      noun

          Your home is very close to the school   (place)

E. Possessive nouns often signal other nouns. They show ownership.

               poss. noun noun   **poss. noun**   **noun**

Examples: **Marilyn's** parrot   **boys'** locker **room**

F. Indefinites include **some**, **any**, **no**, **many**, **few**, **several**, and others. Stop at all indefinites. Check to see if a noun follows it. There may be a few words between the indefinite and the noun.

                        noun

Examples: **Several** tornadoes were spotted.   (things)

                      noun

          No new actresses were hired.   (persons)

Some left early. (*Some* is not a determiner. Some what? No noun is given.)

Several ~~of the loons~~ are gone. *Several* is not a determiner. *Loons* has been crossed out.

108

Name_____

Date_____

Directions: In the space provided, write the underlined determiner and the noun that it modifies (goes over to):

Example: Our family likes to watch old movies.   _____Our family_____

1. The Arctic region is rather cold.   _____

2. Keep your essay in this notebook.   _____

3. We'd like two doughnuts for breakfast.   _____

4. Tina will become a bride in June.   _____

5. May we buy some candy?   _____

6. He has changed his plans again.   _____

7. This machine needs more paper.   _____

8. Have you read Julie's letter?   _____

9. No money was raised for the trip.   _____

10. The ponies' master is kind.   _____

11. They put an ornament on the tree.   _____

12. How do you operate that computer?   _____

13. Our favorite dessert is a brownie.   _____

14. Are many caves found in Kentucky?   _____

15. These sunglasses have been found.   _____

Directions: In the space provided, write the underlined determiner with the noun it modifies (goes over to).

Example: Tree trimmers piled <u>many</u> branches there.   ____many branches____

1.   Please don't take <u>my</u> new shoes.   _____

2.   We found a <u>few</u> grasshoppers.   _____

3.   <u>An</u> award for sportsmanship is given.   _____

4.   Did you see those <u>two</u> large hornets?   _____

5.   <u>Brian's</u> friend is learning to be an umpire.   _____

6.   He removed fat from <u>the</u> piece of meat.   _____

7.   The telephone is in <u>her</u> closet.   _____

8.   You need not do <u>any</u> hard work today.   _____

9.   They haven't been here for <u>several</u> years.   _____

10.   <u>That</u> one-way street has been closed.   _____

11.   In <u>twelve</u> days, we are going to Iowa.   _____

12.   A chipmunk has lost <u>its</u> way.   _____

13.   May I have <u>some</u> mashed potatoes?   _____

14.   A <u>boys'</u> club offered basketball games.   _____

15.   Campers put <u>their</u> gear by the van.   _____

NOUNS

COMMON AND PROPER NOUNS

A common noun refers to any person, place, or thing.
Do not capitalize common nouns.

person: boy   place: zoo   thing: building

A type of something is also a common noun.
A type of building is a bank. A bank is still a common noun.

A proper noun names a specific person, place, or thing.
Capitalize a proper noun.

Common Noun: beach

  Proper Noun: **H**untington **B**each

Common Noun: dog
Common Noun: collie (type of dog--still a common noun)

  Proper Noun: **B**owser (name of a particular dog)

Common Noun: state

  Proper Noun: **N**orth **C**arolina (name of a specific state)

Common Noun: airport

  Proper Noun: **D**ulles **I**nternational **A**irport

Name_____

Date_____

Directions: In the space provided, write a proper noun for each common noun.

Example: creek -_____Beaver Creek_____

1. person - _____

2. street - _____

3. lake - _____

4. park - _____

5. restaurant - _____

6. athlete - _____

7. store - _____

8. river - _____

9. country - _____

10. company - _____

Name- - - - - - - - - - - -

Date _ _ _ _ _ _ _ _ _ _ _ _

Directions: Write <u>C</u> if the noun is a common noun; write <u>P</u> if the noun is a proper noun.

1.   _____   MOUNTAIN

2.   _____   MT.BALDY

3.   _____   JOHN WAYNE

4.   _____   ACTOR

5.   _____   BANK

6.   _____   THUNDERBIRD BANK

7.   _____   RIVER

8.   _____   COLORADO RIVER

9.   _____   PASTOR KLEGG

10.   _____   MINISTER

11.   _____   WRITER

12.   _____   MARK TWAIN

13.   _____   SANDRA DAY O'CONNER

14.   _____   JUDGE

15.   _____   REHOBOTH BEACH

16.   _ _   BEACH

17.   _____   PLANET

18.   _____   SATURN

19.   _____   KANSAS

20.   _____   STATE

21.   _____   PACIFIC OCEAN

22.   _____   OCEAN

23.   _____   ISLAND

24.   _____   HAWAII

25.   _____   TED'S BODY SHOP

26.   _____   SHOP

27.   _____   RACE

28.   _____   INDIANAPOLIS 500

29.   _ _   CIRCUSLAND

30.   _____   PARK

31.   _____   AMY GRANT

32.   _____   SINGER

Name_____

Date_____

Directions: Write <u>C</u> if the noun is a common noun; write <u>P</u> if the noun is a proper noun.

Remember: **A common noun doesn't name a specific person, place or thing. There are usually many of a common noun: dog. Types are still common: poodle.**
A proper noun names a <u>particular</u> person, place, or thing: Fido.

1. _____ FLOWER

2. _____ DAFFODIL

3. _____ SEARS TOWER

4. _____ CUSHION

5. _____ BETSY ROSS

6. _____ GREAT SALT LAKE

7. _____ MOTEL

8. _____ LONDON BRIDGE

9. _____ ENCYCLOPEDIA

10. _____ FAITH CHURCH

11. _____ DR. SABO

12. _____ BAY

13. _____ DIME

14. _____ POST CARD

15. _____ COMB

16. _____ ELM STREET

17. _____ GLEN'S DINER

18. _____ GREENWAY ROAD

19. _____ SALVATION ARMY

20. _____ BALLET

21. _____ FREEDOM TRAIL

22. _____ WALLET

23. _____ SEAMSTRESS

24. _____ GRAND CANYON

25. _____ FLAG

26. _____ MR. ADAMS

27. _____ HEARTHSIDE INN

28. _____ KITE

29. _____ CANADA

30. _____ FAIR

31. _____ LAKE ONTARIO

32. _____ TERRIER

NOUNS

SINGULAR AND PLURAL NOUNS

Singular means one.
Plural means more than one.

Rule 1: **The plural of most nouns is made by adding s to the noun.**

    door/doors   star/stars   window/windows   gate/gates

Rule 2: **When a singular noun ends in s, sh, ch, x, or z, add es to form the plural.**

    gas/gases   dish/dishes   punch/punches   wax/waxes   buzz/buzzes

Rule 3: **When a singular noun ends in a vowel + y, add s to form the plural.**

    bay/bays   guy/guys   toy/toys   monkey/monkeys

Rule 4: **When a singular noun ends in consonant + y, change the y to i and add es to form the plural.**

    strawberry/strawberries   cry/cries   filly/fillies

Rule 5: **Some nouns totally change in the plural form.**

    woman/women   child/children   ox/oxen

    Use a dictionary to check the plural form of nouns. If the word totally changes to form the plural, the dictionary will spell out the plural.
pl. = plural

        Example: tooth (n), pl. teeth - 1. hard, bonelike structure...

Rule 6: **Some nouns are the same in both the singular and plural form.**

        deer/deer   sheep/sheep

Use a dictionary to check the plural form of nouns. If the noun does
not change, the dictionary will show it.

   Example: sheep (n), pl. sheep 1. an ovine animal...

Rule 7: **Some nouns ending in f, change the f to v and add es to form the
plural.**

   leaf/leaves   calf/calves   life/lives

  Use a dictionary to check the plural form of nouns. If there is
a change, the dictionary will show it.

   Example: life (n), pl. lives [ME...] a living being

Rule 8: **Some nouns ending in f, simply add s to form the plural.**

   gulf/gulfs   staff/staffs   huff/huffs

  Use a dictionary to check the plural form of nouns. If s is added,
no special entry (*pl.*) will be given.

Rule 9: **Some nouns ending in o, add s to form the plural.**
   Some nouns ending in o, add es to form the plural.

  Use a dictionary to check the plural form of nouns. If s should
be added, no special plural entry will be given. If es should be added, the
entry with *pl.* will be given.

   Example: tomato (n), pl. *-toes* {Sp...] 1. a red or yellow fruit

Rule 10: **Some hyphenated nouns add s to the first part when forming the
plural. The same applies to some non-hyphenated nouns.**

  Check your dictionary for the correct plural form.

   mother-in-law/mothers-in-law

IMPORTANT NOTE: **If two plural forms are given in a dictionary entry,
the first listed is the more acceptable.**

   Example: cactus (n), pl. cacti, cactuses 1. desert plant

116

Name_____   **NOUNS**
                                                          Plurals
Date_____

Directions: Write the plural form in the space after the noun. In the first space,
              write the number of the rule.

      Example: __4__   berry - _____berries_____

1. _____ post - _____

2. _____ gate - _____

3. _____ toothbrush - _____

4. _____ guy - _____

5. _____ sheep - _____

6. _____ buzz - _____

7. _____ pencil - _____

8. _____ penny - _____

9. _____ child - _____

10. _____ bus - _____

11. _____ box - _____

12. _____ pea - _____

13. _____ calf - _____

14. _____ lunch - _____

15. _____ tomato - _____

Name_____   **NOUNS**
                                              Plurals

Date_____

Directions: Write the plural form in the space after the noun. In the first space,
              write the number of the rule.

        Example: __9__   potato - _____potatoes_____

1. _____   baby - _____

2. _____   page - _____

3. _____   nephew - _____

4. _____   tooth - _____

5. _____   banjo - _____

6. _____   whiff - _____

7. _____   watch - _____

8. _____   clay - _____

9. _____   lesson - _____

10. _____   mess - _____

11. _____   flash - _____

12. _____   goose - _____

13. _____   shrimp - _____

14. _____   tear - _____

15. _____   brother-in-law - _____

Name_____   **NOUNS**
                                                Plurals
Date_____

Directions: Write the plural form in the space after the noun.   In the first space, write
              the number of the rule.

              Example: __1__   ski - _____skis_____

1. _____   ditch - _____

2. _____   play - _____

3. _____   house - _____

4. _____   gulf - _____

5. _____   fern - _____

6. _____   cherry - _____

7. _____   wish - _____

8. _____   mouse - _____

9. _____   class - _____

10. _____   studio - _____

11. _____   greeting - _____

12. _____   thief - _____

13. _____   man - _____

14. _____   fez - _____

15. _____   key - _____

NOUNS

POSSESSIVE NOUNS

RULE A: **To form the possessive of a singular noun, add 's to the noun.**

        Examples: baby + rattle = baby's rattle

                     dog + leash = dog's leash

                     cup + handle = cup's handle

      This rule applies to all singular nouns, even those ending in s.

        Examples: class + teacher = class's teacher

                     Mrs. Jones + son = Mrs. Jones's son

RULE B: **To form the possessive of a plural noun ending in s, add ' after the s.**

        Examples: (more than one boy)   boys' bathroom

                     (more than one horse)   horses' corral

                     (more than one cow)   cows' pasture

RULE C: **To form the possessive of a plural noun that does NOT end in s, add 's to the word.**

        Examples: one woman/two women

                     women's meeting

                     one mouse/two mice

                     mice's hole

Name_____

Date_____

Directions: Write the possessive form.

Example: leader belonging to a few girls: _____girls' leader_____

1. tap shoes belonging to a dancer: _____dancer's shoes_____

2. a cage belonging to two birds: _____~~birds's cage~~_____ birds's cage

3. notes belonging to a student: _____student's notes_____

4. a lounge belonging to all workers: _____workers's lounge_____

5. feathers belonging to a heron: _____heron's feathers_____

6. a banana split belonging to Miss Liss: _____Miss liss's banana split_____

7. a meadow belonging to one deer: _____deer's meadow_____

8. a trail for joggers: _____joggers's trail_____

9. pearls belonging to a princess: _____princess's pearls_____

10. a center for many visitors: _____visiters's center_____

Name_____

Date_____

Directions: Circle any determiner(s). Look for a noun that closely follows each
determiner. Box any noun.

DETERMINERS:
1. a, an, the
2. this, that, those, these
3. numbers: example: fifteen sleeping bags
4. my, his, her, your, its, our, their
5. possessives: example: frog's legs
6. several, few, many, some, any, no

**Reminder: Read each sentence. Then, go back and look for determiners.
When you see a determiner, STOP, and check if a noun is closely
following it.   Say the determiner to yourself and add <u>what</u> to it. If you
can answer, the word that completes the <u>what</u> is a noun.**
Example: That ring is pretty.
That is a possible determiner.
That <u>what?</u>   Answer: that ring
Therefore, *ring* is a noun and should be boxed.
**Next, go through the sentence and decide if there are any nouns that do
not have a determiner. (<u>Not all nouns have determiners in front of them.</u>)**

1. A swallow flew into an orchard.

2. Her gerbil is in the bedroom.

3. Debbie's mother talked to a neighbor.

4. Some cars drove through a tunnel.

5. I made six hamburgers and that salad for lunch.

6. Many children asked their parents for a ride on the Ferris wheel.

7. A parade of five bands and several floats passed by.

8. These jacks and this ball should be put away.

9. The boys' group doesn't have any equipment for the game.

10. Your sister needs this baton for a competition in Philadelphia.

Directions: Circle any determiner(s). Look for a noun that closely follows each determiner. Box any noun.

DETERMINERS:
1. a, an, the
2. this, that, those, these
3. numbers: example: fifteen sleeping bags
4. my, his, her, your, its, our, their
5. possesseives: example- frog's legs
6. several, few, many, some, any, no

Reminder: Read each sentence. Then, go back and look for determiners. When you see a determiner, STOP, and check if a noun is closely following it.   Say the determiner to yourself and add <u>what</u> to it. If you can answer, the word that completes the <u>what</u> is a noun.
          Example: Many buses arrived.
                    Many is a possible determiner.
                    Many <u>what?</u>   Answer: many buses
                    Therefore, *buses* is a noun and should be boxed.
Next, go through the sentence and decide if there are any nouns that do not have a determiner. (<u>Not all nouns have determiners in front of them.</u>)

1. Your television has three knobs.

2. Lennie's cousin has many guppies.

3. Are thirty waiters serving at that luncheon?

4. Their lawn mower has an electric switch.

5. A porcupine's quills are thin with sharp points.

6. Those butterflies spread their wings and flew off.

7. The skeleton's bones have been assembled for science class.

8. Do the secretaries in that office have any vacation days left?

9. During our first summer in this home, we painted my bedroom with a blue paint.

10. Some tourists at the museum asked to see Monet's paintings.

Directions: Circle any determiner(s). Look for a noun that closely follows each determiner. Box any noun.

DETERMINERS:
1. a, an, the
2. this, that, those, these
3. numbers: example: fifteen sleeping bags
4. my, his, her, your, its, our, their
5. possessives: example: frog's legs
6. several, few, many, some, any, no

Reminder: Read each sentence. Then, go back and look for determiners. When you see a determiner, STOP, and check if a noun is closely following it.   Say the determiner to yourself and add <u>what</u> to it. If you can answer, the word that completes the <u>what</u> is a noun.

Example: Two girls laughed.
Two is a possible determiner.
Two <u>what?</u>   Answer: two girls
Therefore, *girls* is a noun and should be boxed.

Next, go through the sentence and decide if there are any nouns that do not have a determiner. (Not all nouns have determiners in front of them.)

1. His answer was written in the first column.

2. Joyann's house has no curtains in the front window.

3. Their mother yelled across the street to her friend.

4. These baskets contain blueberries and bananas.

5. That boy's bicycle has several dents and a hole in its frame.

6. Some parents with small children sat in an open area of the woods.

7. An orange and several lemons are needed for this recipe.

8. Many squirrels gathered nuts for their long winter ahead.

9. A caterpillar crawled up the flower and slid beneath its leaf.

10. They have purchased four ribbons, some lace, and two bolts of silky fabric.

You have learned about predicate nominatives in the verb unit. Let's review. **A predicate nominative is a noun or pronoun that occurs after a linking verb and means the same as the subject.** (In this unit, a P.N. will be a noun.)

Linking Verbs: to feel   to become   to remain
to taste   to seem   to appear
to look   to sound   to stay
to smell   to grow   to be (is, am, are, was, were, be, being, been)

                                P.N.
Example: Ludwig is the best swimmer.

          Proof: The best swimmer is Ludwig.

Remember: To prove the predicate nominative, invert the sentence. Begin with the word(s) after the verb, include the predicate nominative, and, then, go to the beginning of the sentence. This is called inverting the sentence.

Directions: Cross out any prepositional phrase(s). Underline the subject once and the verb/verb phrase twice. Label any predicate nominative-P.N. Write the proof for the predicate nominative on the line provided.

1. Tahiti is a beautiful island in the South Pacific.

    Proof: _____

2. Their favorite baseball player was Ken Griffey, Jr.

    Proof: _____

3. A planet with rings is Saturn.

    Proof: _____

Name_____

Date_____

Directions: Cross out any prepositional phrase(s). Underline the subject once and
the verb/verb phrase twice. Label any predicate nominative-P.N. Write
the proof for the predicate nominative on the line provided.

1.   A green precious gem is an emerald.

Proof: _____

2.   The last person in the race was their teacher.

Proof: _____

3.   A penguin is a flightless bird of the Southern Hemisphere.

Proof: _____

4.   Janeen Holloway is the president of the Aviators' Club.

Proof: _____

5.   Karen's favorite book remains Black Beauty.

Proof: _____

6.   Joe's cousin is the manager of his high school's football team.

Proof: _____

7.   Jody's favorite part of math became fractions.

Proof: _____

128

<u>Direct objects receive the action of the verb.</u>

                             D.O.

Example: <u>He</u> <u>bought</u> a straw hat.   The object he bought is a *hat*.

Sometimes, the direct object is compound (more than one).

                            D.O.   **D.O.**

Example: <u>Volunteers</u> <u>served</u> strawberries and cream ~~at the fund-raiser~~.

Directions: Cross out any prepositional phrase(s). Underline the subject once and
the verb/verb phrase twice. Label any direct object-<u>D.O.</u>

1. Lynnsey received a puppy for her birthday.

2. Ida pushed a penny across the table.

3. The librarian forgot her umbrella today.

4. That typist finished ten letters in an hour.

5. Those pigeons ate all the food in the dog's dish.

6. Patty's mom plays tennis every day.

7. We cleaned the bathroom and the kitchen.

8. Are you buying new clothes for vacation?

9. Misty needed five stitches in her knee.

10. The girl beside me sings different tunes to herself.

11. Gloria wants a new bike and a chain lock with a secret code.

12. Put these tapes and credit cards in a safe place.

NOUNS

Indirect Objects

The indirect object is the receiver of some direct objects.

Example: He handed the clerk ten dollars.

I.O.   D.O.
He <u>handed</u> the **clerk** ten dollars.

RULES FOR INDIRECT OBJECTS:

1. In order to have an indirect object in the sentence, you must have a direct object.

2. You must be able to insert *to* or *for* **mentally** in front of an indirect object.

to   **I.O.**   **D.O.**
Examples: The hotel <u>clerk</u> <u>handed</u> / the guest his key.

for **I.O.**   **D.O.**
Mr. Jackson <u>prepared</u>/ the family his famous chili.

NOTE: If *to* or *for* is actually **written** in the sentence, the noun is not an indirect object.
Example: Mr. Jackson made his famous chili **for** his family.

A. A sentence containing a direct object does not always contain an indirect object.

D.O.
Examples: The <u>florist</u> <u>delivered</u> flowers.   (no indirect object)

I.O. **D.O.**
The <u>florist</u> <u>delivered</u> Hannah flowers.   (indirect object)

B. Some sentences may contain compound indirect objects.

I.O.   **I.O.**   **D.O.**
Example: Ty's <u>mother</u> <u>made</u> Ginger and her brother some fudge.

130

Directions: Read each sentence. Decide if you could **mentally** insert *to* or *for* above the slash (/). Write *to* or *for*, whichever makes sense, on the line.

1. Bill handed ___/ Mrs. Johnson papers.

2. Aunt Vestal has quilted ___/ her niece a small blanket.

3. Dad handed ___/ Mom a wrench for the sink.

4. That graphic artist designed ___/ the company a logo.

5. The usher handed ___/ Jerry and Nicki colorful programs.

Directions: Cross out any prepositional phrase(s). Underline the subject once and the verb/verb phrase twice. Label a direct object-D.O. and an indirect object-I.O.

I.O.   D.O.
Example: The <u>mayor</u> <u><u>presented</u></u> her the key ~~to the city~~.

1. Bill handed Mrs. Johnson papers.

2. Aunt Vestal has quilted her niece a small blanket.

3. Dad handed Mom a wrench for the sink.

4. That graphic artist designed the company a logo.

5. The usher handed Jerry and Nicki colorful programs.

Directions: Read each sentence. Decide if you could mentally insert *to* or *for* above the slash (/). Write *to* or *for*, whichever makes sense, on the line.

1. That company provides ‾‾‾ / its salespeople a car.

2. Miss Anders sent ‾‾‾ / her nephew a statue from Peru.

3. The parcel service delivers ‾‾‾ / Dad packages of books.

4. His sister baked ‾‾‾ / her church group some brownies.

5. Marshall makes ‾‾‾ / his family breakfast every morning.

Directions: Cross out any prepositional phrase(s). Underline the subject once and the verb/verb phrase twice. Label a direct object-D.O. and an indirect object-I.O.

                         I.O.   **D.O.**

Example: <u>Ken</u> <u>ironed</u> Melissa a blouse.

1. That company provides its salespeople a car.

2. Miss Anders sent her nephew a statue from Peru.

3. The parcel service delivers Dad packages of books.

4. His sister baked her church group some brownies.

5. Marshall makes his family breakfast every morning.

NOUNS
Indirect Objects

Directions: Cross out any prepositional phrase(s). Underline the subject once and the verb/verb phrase twice. Label a direct object-D.O. and an indirect object-I.O.

                               I.O.   **D.O.**
Example: The <u>clown</u> <u>gave</u> the children some popcorn.

1. Sandy gave her friend a bracelet.

2. The waitress handed Mom the bill.

3. Scott gave Jill a ring for an engagement present.

4. The girl in the back row passes her friends notes.

5. That barber gives his customers free combs.

6. I shall bake my friends a cherry cake with cream cheese icing.

7. A zoo keeper fed the lions their daily food.

8. The coach gave each boy a trophy.

9. A carnival attendant handed the boy three balls for the game.

10. Hand the food seller this dollar for a cola.

Name_____

Date_____

A. Directions: Write <u>A</u> if the noun is abstract; write <u>C</u> if the noun is concrete.

1. _____   sock   5. _____   tin

2. _____   brick   6. _____   love

3. _____   hope   7. _____   blossom

4. _____   polish   8. _____   air

B. Directions: Write <u>C</u> if the noun is common; write <u>P</u> if the noun is proper.

1. _____   BIRD   5. _____   LINCOLN SCHOOL

2. _____   ROBIN   6. _____   GOLDEN GATE BRIDGE

3. _____   BUILDING   7. _____   BOOK

4. _____   SCHOOL   8. _____   ROANOKE ISLAND

C. Directions: Write <u>A</u> if the underlined word serves as an adjective (describing
                  word); write <u>N</u> if the underlined word serves as a noun.

1. _____   They enjoy working on their <u>computer</u>.

2. _____   Mrs. Jamison is a <u>computer</u> programmer.

3. _____   Please sit on the <u>carpet</u> and talk to us.

4. _____   Grandmother has an antique <u>carpet</u> beater.

5. _____   The young woman wore a striped <u>hair</u> band.

6. _____   Her <u>hair</u> had been dyed a golden blonde with brown highlights.

7. _____   The <u>ceiling</u> fan helps to cool the house in the summer.

8. _____   Some flies were walking across the <u>ceiling</u> of the old shed.

D. Directions: Write <u>V</u> if the underlined word serves as a verb; write <u>N</u> if the underlined word serves as a noun.

1. _____   The man began his <u>washing</u> after he came home from work.

2. _____   Are you <u>washing</u> the floors before you leave for vacation?

3. _____   Mr. and Mrs. Fisher enjoyed the <u>talk</u> about New Zealand.

4. _____   Did Congressman Keats <u>talk</u> to the class today?

E. Write the plural:

1. fence - _____   6. library - _____

2. eyelash - _____   7. list - _____

3. half - _____   8. hunch - _____

4. mix - _____   9. moose - _____

5. boy - _____   10. peach - _____

F. Directions: Write the possessive form.

1. a net belonging to a fisherman: _____

2. food belonging to James: _____

3. a vase for some flowers: _____

4. a herd of cattle led by ranchers: _____

5. kittens belonging to an elderly lady: _____

6. a company owned by five men: _____

G.   Directions: Write the determiner and the noun in the space provided.

1.   My relatives live there.   _____

2.   Jennifer's professor is coming.   _____

3.   Have you seen a pyramid?   _____

4.   Many cases had been decided.   _____

5.   That suitcase is new.   _____

6.   I would like two brownies.   _____

7.   He sold me these boots.   _____

H.   Directions: Box any nouns.

1.   Jeremy placed two straws in his soda.

2.   His mother wiped the stain from the jacket.

3.   Two tall trees with white lights stood in ceramic containers.

4.   Several silk ties were reduced to ten dollars at the department store.

5.   Her love for her children is shown in her kind speech and gentleness.

6.   The grocer delivers our milk and bread to our home each week.

Name_____   **CUMULATIVE REVIEW**

Date_____

A. Directions: List 50 prepositions.

1. _____   14. _____   27. _____   40. _____

2. _____   15. _____   28. _____   41. _____

3. _____   16. _____   29. _____   42. _____

4. _____   17. _____   30. _____   43. _____

5. _____   18. _____   31. _____   44. _____

6. _____   19. _____   32. _____   45. _____

7. _____   20. _____   33. _____   46. _____

8. _____   21. _____   34. _____   47. _____

9. _____   22. _____   35. _____   48. _____

10. _____   23. _____   36. _____   49. _____

11. _____   24. _____   37. _____   50. _____

12. _____   25. _____   38. _____

13. _____   26. _____   39. _____

B. Directions: Cross out any prepositional phrase(s). Underline the subject once
    and the verb/verb phrase twice.

1. A scarf was wrapped around her head.

2. During the dust storm, some cars did not pull off the road.

3. He walked in among the fans and sat down.

4. Jonathan and his mom waited at the airport for two hours.

5. One of the workers had gone to a local market to buy chips.

137

C. Directions: List the 23 helping (auxiliary) verbs:

_____

_____

_____

D. Directions: Cross out any prepositional phrase(s).   Underline the subject once
and the verb/verb phrase twice.   Label any direct object-<u>D.O.</u>

1. A clerk dropped a dollar on the floor.

2. Sean wants a puppy for his birthday.

3. Their dentist gave toothbrushes to them.

4. Millicent sings lullabies to her baby at night.

5. The butler showed the guests to the huge dining room.

6. The masons finished the wall after sundown.

7. Please empty that trash can into the huge dumpster.

E. Directions: Cross out any prepositional phrase(s).   Underline the subject once
and the verb/verb phrase twice.

1. The French designer has (chose, chosen) a new print.

2. His brother has (ridden, rode) his motorcycle today.

3. They had (swam, swum) across the pool three times.

4. Have you (drank, drunk) from this cup?

5. Jacob's meal had been (brought, brung) to him.

6. The city bus should have (come, came) by noon.

F. Directions: Cross out any prepositional phrase(s). Underline the subject once and the verb/verb phrase twice.

1. The listener (sits, sets) with his hands on his head.

2. A tourist (lay, laid) his camera on the seat of the bus.

3. (Sit, Set) your foot on this board.

4. Those cinnamon buns are (raising, rising) in the pantry.

5. Her robe is (lying, laying) by the bed.

6. Charlotte (lies, lays) on a hammock often.

7. Has Mr. Charter (raised, risen) money for his club?

8. Those triplets have (laid, lain) on a raft in the water for an hour.

G. Directions: List the 20 linking verbs (12 infinitives + 8):

_____

_____

H. Directions: Cross out any prepositional phrase(s). Underline the subject once and the verb twice. Write <u>A</u> if the verb is action; write <u>L</u> if the verb is linking.

Remember: If you can place *is, am, are, was,* or *were* above the verb without changing the sentence meaning, it is usually a linking verb.
                                          was
       Example: __L__   His <u>aunt</u> <u>became</u> a journalist.

1. _____   The sea remained calm throughout the day.

2. _____   That child smelled the flowers along the path.

3. _____   My Mexican food tastes too hot for me to eat.

4. _____   The witness answered all the questions quietly.

Name_____

Date_____

I. Directions: Cross out any prepositional phrase(s). Underline the subject once and the verb/verb phrase twice. Label any predicate nominative-P.N. Write the proof on the line.

1. Margaret was the leader of her club.

Proof: _____

2. Her best friend is the boy in the red sweater.

Proof: _____

3. *Spring Party* by Janet Fish became Mom's favorite artwork.

Proof: _____

4. Mr. Sanders remained the president of that organization for four years.

Proof: _____

J. Directions: Cross out any prepositional phrase(s). Underline the subject once and the verb twice. Label any predicate adjective-P.A. Write the predicate adjective and the subject of the sentence on the line provided.

1. The little red wagon is old.   _____

2. Her ruffled blouse is white.   _____

3. His shirt is blue with green stripes.   _____

4. Those boys in black jackets seem

nervous about their performance.   _____

140

Name_____   **CUMULATIVE REVIEW**

Date_____

K. Directions: Write the contraction.

1. it is - _____   6. he would - _____

2. we are - _____   7. you will - _____

3. will not - _____   8. I have - _____

4. what is - _____   9. could not - _____

5. cannot - _____   10. I will - _____

L. Directions: Cross out any prepositional phrase(s). Underline the subject once
    and the verb/verb phrase twice. Determine the tense and write
    present, *past*, or *future* in the space provided.

1. _____ I shall not decide until Monday.

2. _____ The patient reads magazines in the doctor's
                             office.

3. _____ A grocery clerk handed us our bags.

4. _____ We watch whales from a pier.

5. _____ Lance and Stephani made pizza for everyone.

6. _____ That real estate agent sells homes in my area.

7. _____ Cy's family will never forget their trip to
                             Arkansas.

M. Directions: Write *conj.* above any conjunction; write *intj.* above any interjection.

1. Wow! Andy and I had never seen an Egyptian tomb or a mummy!

2. Yikes! This cliff is steep, but we will make it.

141

ADJECTIVES

There are two general types of adjectives: descriptive adjectives and limiting adjectives.

A. **Descriptive adjectives** are describing words. They often tell what kind.

Examples:	**pumpkin** pie	What kind of pie? pumpkin pie
	soft, **velvet** dress	What kind of dress? soft dress
		velvet dress
	red sponge ball	What kind of ball? red ball
		sponge ball

B. **Limiting adjectives** include determiners. Determiners are actually called determining adjectives. These must be memorized and learned.

1. **Determining adjectives**:
    a. Articles: **a, an, the**
    b. Demonstratives: **this, that, those, these**
    c. **Numbers**: twenty-five days   third base
    d. Possessive pronouns (used as adjectives): **my, his, her, its, your, our, their**
    e. **Possessive nouns** (used as adjectives): Niki's cow   teachers' meeting
    f. Indefinites: **many, some, few, several, no, any**...

2. In order to be a determining adjective, <u>a noun must follow it</u>. A determining (also called limiting) adjective modifies a noun. Modifies means *goes over to*.

    Examples: Several laser printers were purchased.

    Several is an adjective because it modifies or goes over to printers. (*Several* what? several printers)

    She had been hired as an architect.

    <u>An</u> is an adjective because it modifies or goes over to architect.   (a/*an* what? an architect)

When a word that may serve as a limiting adjective does not modify a noun, that word serves as a pronoun.

That is funny? *That* is not an adjective. *That* what? We don't know; there is no noun. Therefore, *that* is a pronoun.

Name_____

Date_____

Directions: In the space provided, write the italicized limiting adjective(s) with the noun that it modifies (goes to).

Example: Do you have *any* paper? _____any paper_____

1. *Two* alligators swam through deep water. _____

2. Do you have a *few* dollars to loan me? _____

3. Please bring *your* swimsuit with you. _____

4. A *boys'* club was begun there. _____

5. Has Mrs. Little seen *these* new shoes? _____

6. They floated down *the* river on rafts. _____

7. *An* apple is filled with pectin. _____

8. Sometimes, he has *no* patience. _____

9. Hand me *that* basket of fruit, please. _____

10. *His* jeep is in *the* parking lot. _____

_____

11. *Jay's* toads are in *a* special garden. _____

_____

12. Have you seen *my* binoculars? _____

13. Chad paid *fifteen* dollars for *a* ticket. _____

_____

14. *This* gum smells like spearmint. _____

Name_____

Date_____

Directions: In the space provided, write the italicized limiting adjective with the noun that it modifies (goes to).

Example: Kimberly left *her* bowl on the table.   ____her bowl____

1. *Charlene's* mouse is cute.   _____

2. *A* free pass was given to him.   _____

3. Have you taken *her* napkin?   _____

4. *This* broken watch must be returned.   _____

5. Wait *twenty* minutes for us.   _____

6. *Several* children played happily.   _____

7. I don't want *my* dessert.   _____

8. The *girls'* dad listened carefully.   _____

9. The teacher requested *an* answer immediately.   _____

10. Did *any* telephone operator stay late?   _____

11. *Those* apricots are spoiled.   _____

12. She reached up for *some* cookies.   _____

13. An eagle spread *its* wings and flew off.   _____

14. Please give Allen *these* sandals.   _____

15. *The* computer chip is very tiny.   _____

144

Name_____

Date_____

Directions: Write <u>A</u> in the first space if the underlined word is an adjective; write <u>P</u> if the underlined word is a pronoun. After the sentence, write the limiting adjective and the noun it modifies.   After <u>P</u>, the line will be blank.

Examples: <u>A</u> <u>Her</u> shampoo is all gone. _____her shampoo_____

<u>P</u> Will you go with <u>her</u>? _____

1. _____ <u>This</u> orange is sour. _____

2. _____ Do you want <u>this</u>? _____

3. _____ I'll take a <u>few</u>! _____

4. _____ He ate a <u>few</u> pancakes. _____

5. _____ <u>Forty</u> came to the reunion. _____

6. _____ There are <u>forty</u> jellybeans in this jar. _____

7. _____ Margie said that she doesn't have <u>any</u>. _____

8. _____ Has Doug bought <u>any</u> caramels? _____

9. _____ <u>That</u> is funny. _____

10. _____ Tell me <u>that</u> joke again. _____

11. _____ Take <u>two</u> with you. _____

12. _____ The baby has <u>two</u> teeth. _____

13. _____ <u>Several</u> will be elected. _____

14. _____ <u>Several</u> blueberry muffins were eaten. _____

ADJECTIVES

There are two general types of adjectives: limiting adjectives and descriptive adjectives.

Descriptive Adjectives:

1. Descriptive adjectives **describe**: yellow, large, plain

2. Descriptive adjectives answer the question **WHAT KIND**.

   Example: stale bread   What kind of bread? *stale*

3. Some suffixes help to identify descriptive adjectives:

   a. **able** - believable, capable, reliable
   b. **al** - critical, unusual
   c. **ar** - muscular, regular
   d. **ible** - digestible, responsible
   e. **ic** - fantastic, basic
   f. **ive** - festive, sensitive
   g. **ful** - playful, careful, colorful
   h. **less** - careless, restless
   i. **ous** - delicious, spacious, luscious
   j. **some** - handsome, burdensome

(Always look for a noun following words with these endings. Some words ending with these suffixes will not serve as adjectives.)

Descriptive adjectives modify (go over to) a noun (or pronoun).

1. Descriptive adjectives often come before the noun or pronoun.

   Examples: A **red** carnation was given to Sue.
   Red describes carnation.

   This **gas** lamp still works.
   Gas describes lamp.

2. Descriptive adjectives sometimes come after the noun or pronoun.

   Examples: His leg, **swollen** and **cut**, was treated for minor injuries.

   This syrup is very **watery**.   (predicate adjective)

146

Directions: First, read each sentence.   Circle any limiting adjective(s).   Then, reread each sentence and circle any describing adjective(s).

1.   Her second child takes jazz dancing.

2.   Derek's friend has brown wavy hair.

3.   A cherry ice drink costs seventy-five cents.

4.   Have you found a small silver bracelet?

5.   The girls' cocker spaniel has black fur.

6.   Later, we ate several toasted marshmallows.

7.   Their cheerful smiles welcomed the tired visitors.

8.   On the next rainy day, we will make chocolate pudding.

9.   Tom's cousin made a silly face at the upset girls.

10.   The hot fudge sundae was topped with whipping cream.

11.   Our last basketball game was long but fun.

12.   An elegant dress with blue sequins was purchased for the holiday party.

Name_____

Date_____

Directions: First, read each sentence. Circle any limiting adjective(s). Then, reread each sentence and circle any describing adjective(s).

1.   Anne's first fruit drink contained ice cubes and pink lemonade.

2.   Spicy food is always a treat in Kerry's family.

3.   Miss Sills wore a fashionable cotton jacket with green stripes.

4.   That old road has dangerous curves and high shoulders.

5.   This coconut cream pie is good but watery.

6.   That group ate raspberry sugarless popsicles.

7.   Seventeen beautiful girls sang in the charity show.

8.   A young girl wrote a special letter to her elderly great aunt.

9.   Several shiny silver dollars were given to an eighth grader.

10.   Their favorite toy is a sponge football with bright stars.

11.   A tall, thin man was sleeping under the weeping willow tree.

12.   Many gorgeous ponies are being shown at the annual firemen's carnival.

Name_____

Date_____

Directions: Circle any adjectives.

Remember: **Search for any limiting adjective(s) first. Then, reread the sentence and find any descriptive adjective(s).**

1. Their blue bike is old and rusty.

2. The quiet child sat near a wide, open window.

3. Mrs. Kilper's short speech included colorful slides of tropical fish.

4. Many cheering fans sat on the comfortable padded benches.

5. The businessman, happy and rested, made notes on his yellow legal pad.

6. Your favorite actor will be appearing at an expensive charity ball.

7. A small yellow canary fluttered among those leafless branches.

8. A brightly colored kimono was given as a Christmas gift to his older sister.

9. A lovely christening outfit had been knitted for their new baby.

10. My festive decorations included green crepe paper and foil streamers.

11. Several diamond rings had been stolen by a short, blonde woman.

12. Have you traded five baseball cards for that valuable autographed copy?

149

ADJECTIVES

Proper Adjectives

A proper adjective is a descriptive word derived from a proper noun.

Proper nouns are capitalized; therefore, proper adjectives are capitalized.

A. Often, a proper adjective will be similar to the proper noun:

PROPER NOUN	PROPER ADJECTIVE	
Japan	Japanese	(Japanese gardens)
Canada	Canadian	(Canadian bacon)
Arab	Arabian	(Arabian horses)

B. Some proper adjectives will be very different from the proper noun:

PROPER NOUN	PROPER ADJECTIVE	
Switzerland	Swiss	(Swiss chocolate)
Holland	Dutch	(Dutch tulips)

C. Sometimes, the proper adjective is the same as the proper noun:

PROPER NOUN	PROPER ADJECTIVE	
Starshine	Starshine	(Starshine coffee)
Tanner House	Tanner House	(Tanner House candles)
Scottsdale	Scottsdale	(Scottsdale police)

Name_____

Date_____

Directions: Underline any proper adjective. Capitalize it.   In the space provided,
write the proper adjective and the noun it modifies (goes to).

                     N   J

Example: They went to a <u>new jersey</u> amusement park. ____New Jersey park____

1. The arizona flag has a large star. _____

2. A french poodle is for sale. _____

3. Granny made a christmas dinner. _____

4. Do you like swiss cheese? _____

5. John's father lives in an italian village. _____

6. That los angeles store offers discounts. _____

7. Have you ridden a new york subway? _____

8. Uncle Fred has learned to make mexican
tortillas. _____

9. A sears catalog came in the mail today. _____

10. We are invited to a greek wedding. _____

Name_____

Date_____

Directions: Underline any proper adjective. Capitalize it. In the space provided,
              write the proper adjective and the noun it modifies (goes to).

                          S   F

Example: Have you seen a <u>san francisco</u> trolley?   _____San Francisco trolley_____

1. We went to an easter service.   _____

2. Alva went to a canadian wilderness
    to photograph moose.   _____

3. Tara attended a hawaiian luau.   _____

4. Did you attend a st. patrick's party?   _____

5. Is there an atlanta football team?   _____

6. Have you seen alaskan king crab?   _____

7. Kameo enjoys regal yogurt.   _____

8. His friend lives in a maine apartment.   _____

9. Mira goes to the african nation of Egypt.   _____

10. The Lopez family loves jewish rye
     bread.   _____

Name_____ **ADJECTIVES**

Date_____

Directions: Read each sentence. First, circle limiting adjectives. Then, circle descriptive adjectives. Be sure to circle proper adjectives.

1. A Boston rocker is for sale at that antique shop.

2. The Edison home is on a quiet street in Ohio.

3. Has your uncle seen the new Regency truck?

4. They chose a pink Valentine's Day card for their friend.

5. For breakfast, we ate scrambled eggs and crisp Canadian bacon.

6. Some enthusiastic people talked eagerly about Sargent's painting.

7. Paco's youngest nephew works on a southern Kansas farm.

8. Amora iced tea was served with fat lemon wedges.

9. An old oak table was topped with a white lace tablecloth and clear crystal goblets.

10. Several Danish sweet rolls and assorted fresh fruit are available in the next room.

11. Santa's helpers were dressed in short red velvet dresses and green tennis shoes.

12. A tall, confused man asked the grocer for directions to the Chinese food aisle.

13. Two college roommates attending their class party had made a lasting friendship.

ADJECTIVES

Predicate Adjectives

A predicate adjective is a describing word that occurs in the predicate of the sentence and describes the subject.

The predicate starts at the verb and goes to the end of the sentence.

Examples: Mary <u>likes</u> to ride her bike in the park.

likes to ride her bike in the park = predicate

The man in the blue tie <u>lives</u> near me.

lives near me = predicate

Steps in identifying a predicate adjective:

1. Look for a linking verb. A predicate adjective will occur after a linking verb.

Linking verbs:	to feel	to appear	to sound
	to taste	to become	to stay
	to look	to grow	to be (is, am, are, was,
	to smell	to remain	were, be, being, been)

Remember: To check for a linking verb, try replacing the verb with a form of <u>to be</u>:

is, am, are, was, or *were*.   If you can do this without changing the meaning of the sentence, the verb is usually linking.

Examples: Joe **<u>looks</u>** happy today.

Joe **<u>is</u>** happy today.

The shopper **<u>became</u>** concerned about her lost child.

The shopper **<u>was</u>** concerned about her lost child.

154

2. If the sentence contains a linking verb, check if a word in the predicate describes the subject. The adjective must describe the subject, not another word in the predicate.

P.A.

Examples: That <u>girl</u> <u>is</u> very funny.   (funny girl)

(funny = predicate adjective)

His <u>dad</u> <u>was</u> a silver medal winner.

(*Silver* occurs in the predicate. However, *silver* describes winner. Dad is not silver! Therefore, *silver* is not a predicate adjective.)

3. If there is a linking verb and the adjective in the predicate (after the verb) describes the subject, the word is a predicate adjective.

This soup tastes delicious.

P.A.

This <u>soup</u> <u>tastes</u> delicious.   (delicious soup)

NOTE: A question (interrogative sentence) usually has the predicate adjective and the noun after the verb.

Is your bathroom clean?

To determine a predicate adjective more easily, change the question to a statement.

Your bathroom is clean.

Then, go through the steps by asking the following questions:
1. Is there a possible linking verb?
2. Is there an adjective in the predicate (after the verb)?
3. Does the adjective in the predicate go back and describe the subject?

P.A.

Your <u>bathroom</u> <u>is</u> clean.   (clean bathroom)

Use this method to help identify any predicate adjective. However, be sure to change a question to a statement first.

Date_____

Directions: Cross out any prepositional phrase(s). Underline the subject once and
the verb/verb phrase twice. Label any predicate adjective-_P.A._ Write the
predicate adjective and the noun it modifies on the line provided.

P.A.

Example: His <u>pliers</u> <u>are</u> rusty. _____rusty pliers_____

1. The baseball shoes are black. _____

2. Those tarts taste sweet. _____

3. Her hair had been kinky. _____

4. This pickle tastes sweet. _____

5. Your voice seems hoarse from yelling. _____

6. The man remained silent. _____

7. The drawer is full of old clothes. _____

8. Your face appears swollen. _____

9. That horn sounds too loud. _____

10. The dog grew excited by the stranger's
voice. _____

Name_____

Date_____

Directions: Cross out any prepositional phrase(s). Underline the subject once and the verb/verb phrase twice. Label any predicate adjective-P.A. Write the predicate adjective and the noun it modifies on the line provided.

                                         P.A.
    Example: The <u>crackers</u> ~~in the soup~~ <u><u>are</u></u> mushy.   mushy crackers

1. His thumb was feeling numb.   _____

2. The edge of that knife is sharp.   _____

3. Her foot became enlarged from the
    spider bite.   _____

4. A waitress appeared upset by the
    customer's remark.   _____

5. That riverbed is dry again.   _____

6. His hair is blonde.   _____

7. After the argument, the two ladies

    were friendly.   _____

8. Their socks had become holey.   _____

9. Throughout the winter, the walks had

    remained icy.   _____

10. Her finger became sore around the
    joint.   _____

ADJECTIVES

Degrees of Adjectives

Adjectives are used to make comparisons.

    A. The **comparative form** compares **two**.

    B. The **superlative form** compares **three or more**.

      Examples: This thumb nail is <u>shorter</u> than my index finger nail.

                  Of all the nails, the thumb nail is <u>shortest</u>.

There are several ways to form the comparative and superlative forms:

    A. **Comparative**:

        1. Add <u>**er**</u> to most one-syllable adjectives:

             low/lower   strong/stronger

        2. Add <u>**er**</u> to some two-syllable adjectives:

             sincere/sincerer   pretty/prettier

        3. Place <u>**more**</u> (or less) before some two-syllable adjectives:

             famous/more famous   special/more special

  IMPORTANT: **Use your DICTIONARY to determine if <u>er</u> should be added to a two-syllable adjective.**

        4. Before adjectives of three or more syllables, add <u>**more**</u> (or less) to make comparisons.

158   responsible/more responsible   expensive/more expensive

5. Some adjectives completely change form.

   good/better   bad/worse

B. Superlative:

1. Add **est** to most one-syllable adjectives:

   low/lowest   strong/strongest

2. Add **est** to some two-syllable adjectives:

   sincere/sincerest   pretty/prettiest

3. Place **most** (or least) before some two-syllable adjectives:

   famous/most famous   special/most special

IMPORTANT: **Use a DICTIONARY to determine if est should be added to a two-syllable adjective.**

4. Place **most** (or least) before three-syllable adjectives.

   responsible/most responsible   expensive/most expensive

5. Some adjectives totally change form.

   good/best   bad/worst

Remember:

1. **Use the comparative form when comparing 2 items.**

   Example: He is friendlier than his sister.

2. **Use the superlative form when comparing 3 items or more.**

   Example: He is tallest of the five boys.

Name_____

Date_____

Directions: Write the required comparative or superlative form of the given adjective
in the space provided.

Example: comparative form of beautiful - _____more beautiful_____

1. comparative form of lively -   _____

2. superlative form of sticky -   _____

3. comparative form of fast -   _____

4. superlative form of disinterested - _____

5. comparative form of creative -   _____

6. comparative form of dull -   _____

7. superlative form of thrilling -   _____

8. comparative form of dangerous -   _____

9. comparative form of white -   _____

10. superlative form of happy -   _____

Name_____

Date_____

Directions: Write the required comparative or superlative form of the given adjective
in the space provided.

Example: superlative form of wise - _____wisest_____

1.   comparative form of small -   _____

2.   superlative form of honest -   _____

3.   comparative form of angry -   _____

4.   comparative form of careless -   _____

5.   superlative form of good -   _____

6.   superlative form of courageous -   _____

7.   comparative form of delicious -   _____

8.   comparative form of funny -   _____

9.   superlative form of hard -   _____

10.   superlative form of careless -   _____

Directions: Choose the correct form in each sentence.

Example: His uncle is (taller, **tallest**) of that singing trio.

1.   This watermelon is (bigger, biggest) than that one.

2.   That cucumber is (largest, larger) of all the ones in the bin.

3.   My barbecue sandwich is (tastier, tastiest) than the one I ate yesterday.

4.   The whirlpool tub is (deeper, deepest) than the regular one.

5.   Mrs. Yales is (taller, tallest) than her sister.

6.   The drawer at the bottom is (more spacious, most spacious) of the entire chest.

7.   Those twins are cute; however, the taller one is (more demanding, most demanding).

8.   This pack of football cards is (badder, worse) than your pack.

9.   Is the Atlantic Ocean (more peaceful, most peaceful) than the Pacific Ocean?

10.   Her living room is the (fancier, fanciest) room of the entire house.

11.   Of the two brothers, Harvey is (younger, youngest).

12.   This painting is (more abstract, most abstract) of all the ones in the museum.

13.   Miss Shales is the (more talkative, most talkative) woman in her college class.

14.   This blue wagon is (smaller, smallest) than the red wagon that was given away.

15.   Of the four girls, Jolene is the (more energetic, most energetic).

Name_____

Date_____

Directions: Choose the correct form in each sentence.

        Example: That wrench is (**older**, oldest) than this hammer.

1. This paper is (shorter, shortest) than the regular size.

2. This floor is (dirtier, dirtiest) than it was yesterday.

3. Mike is the (more comical, most comical) member of that comedy club.

4. This horse is (gentler, gentlest) of all the horses in the barn.

5. He wanted the (better, best) shirt on the rack.

6. Laura chose the (heavier, heaviest) bowling ball at the alley.

7. That old car is (more dependable, most dependable) than this new one.

8. Which choir member do you think is (more talented, most talented)?

9. That salesman was (friendlier, friendliest) of all conference attendees.

10. Of all the balls in the bin, this one is (more inflated, most inflated).

11. Joanne and Troy have the (cuter, cutest) cat in the neighborhood.

12. The small parrot seems (noisier, noisiest) than the large one.

13. Mandy's school pictures are (prettier, prettiest) than last year's pictures.

14. Mrs. Jamison is wearing the (more beautiful, most beautiful) dress at the dance.

15. Is Mel the (more daring, most daring) diver you have ever seen?

Name_____

Date_____

A. Directions: In the space provided, write the underlined adjective with the noun
    that it modifies (goes over to).

    Example: Does <u>his</u> shirt need to be ironed? _____his shirt_____

1. Do you have <u>any</u> juice? _____

2. <u>These</u> nuts are too salty. _____

3. Will you hand me <u>an</u> orange? _____

4. Is this <u>your</u> yellow sweater? _____

5. <u>Penny's</u> laugh is very loud. _____

6. <u>Several</u> leasing agents helped everyone. _____

7. I'll take <u>three</u> hard pretzels, please. _____

B. Directions: Write <u>A</u> in the space provided if the underlined word is an adjective;
    write <u>P</u> if the underlined word is a pronoun (stands alone). After the
    sentence, write the limiting adjective and the noun it modifies.
    (After <u>P</u>, the line will be blank.)

    Example: __A__ <u>This</u> desk is maple. _____This desk_____

              __P__ <u>This</u> is easy. _____

1. _____ Do you want <u>these</u> marbles? _____

2. _____ I found <u>these</u> in the closet. _____

3. _____ Have <u>many</u> been invited? _____

4. _____ <u>Many</u> flowers are in bloom. _____

5. _____ Would you like <u>one</u>? _____

6. _____ I want <u>one</u> ice cream cone. _____

164

Name_____

Date_____

C. Directions: Underline any proper adjective and capitalize it. In the space provided, write the proper adjective and the noun it modifies.

                                    M

       Example: Dora went to a <u>missouri</u> town.   __Missouri town__

1. They rode bikes along a california beach.   _____

2. Their family ate at a houston deli.   _____

3. Tate lives near a mexican restaurant.   _____

4. Does he go to a doggymart store?   _____

5. They are part of a rocky mountain hiking team.   _____

6. The lady purchased lipsco crackers today. _____

D. Directions: Cross out any prepositional phrase(s). Underline the subject once and the verb/verb phrase twice. Label any predicate adjective-<u>P.A.</u> Write the predicate adjective and the noun it modifies on the line.

                                      P.A.

      Example: The <u>pillars</u> ~~in this museum~~ <u><u>are</u></u> high.   __high pillars__

1. The sky remained dark during the storm.   _____

2. An Arizona sunset is colorful.   _____

3. Those sidewalks are icy near the edges.   _____

4. His friend's mom seems fearful of some dogs.   _____

5. My answer was very careless.   _____

6. His back became quite sunburned .   _____

7. Her bracelet became rusty from water.   _____

Name_____

Date_____

E. Directions: Circle any adjectives.

Remember: **First circle any limiting adjective(s). Next, circle descriptive adjective(s).**

1. A fake fur hat was worn by a German woman.

2. The brown carpeting is being replaced by marble tile.

3. Several lovable retrievers played near the French doors.

4. Has his youngest cousin ever gone to that water park?

5. Kyle's car was taken across a peaceful lake by that ferry boat.

6. Their carved glass plate is in a lighted china cupboard.

7. The delicious lunch consists of a sliced beef sandwich, two celery sticks, and an egg roll.

F. Directions: Choose the correct form.

1. I think this plaid scarf is (prettier, more pretty) than the striped one.

2. This groomer is (patienter, more patient) than his assistant.

3. Your foot is (longer, longest) than mine.

4. Jay's cousin is (most determined, more determined) to win than Jay is.

5. The employee received an award for being the (more dependable, most dependable) reservationist in the entire office.

6. Of their family, she is (more helpful, most helpful) to her grandfather.

7. Shirley's suitcase is (more durable, most durable) than her duffel bag.

8. This is the (better, best) handwriting example in the entire book.

Name_____   **CUMULATIVE REVIEW**

Date_____

A. Directions: Cross out any prepositional phrase(s). Underline the subject once
and the verb/verb phrase twice. Label any direct object-D.O.

1. Everyone except the man in the back row left the theater.

2. Len tossed the frisbee past his sister and her friend.

3. The women prepared dinner and read for an hour.

4. We collect shells and small pebbles at the beach.

5. Take this empty box to the garbage can.
....
B. Directions: Cross out any prepositional phrase(s). Underline the subject once
and the verb/verb phrase twice. Label any direct object-D.O. Label
any indirect object-I.O.

1. The father gave his son ten dollars.

2. A florist designed the new store a huge silk arrangement.

3. We sent Grandma tickets to visit.

4. He will make Jonathan a new outfit.

....
C. Directions: List the 23 helping verbs: _____

_____
....
D. Directions: Cross out any prepositional phrase(s). Underline the subject once
and the verb/verb phrase twice.

1. The man has (rode, ridden) the camel across the desert.

2. Have you (brought, brung) your skates with you?

3. They should have (flew, flown) earlier.

4. His sister-in-law might have (went, gone) to the zoo.

5. The joggers must have (ran, run) for an hour.   167

Name_____

Date_____

E.   Directions: Cross out any prepositional phrase(s). Underline the subject once and the verb/verb phrase twice. Write the helping verb(s) and the main verb in the correct column.

	helping verb(s)	main verb
1. Mr. Lindner has chosen a new office.	_____	_____
2. I shall leave in the morning.	_____	_____
3. This balloon is leaking.	_____	_____
4. She cannot take anyone to the station.	_____	_____

F.   Directions: Cross out any prepositional phrase(s). Underline the subject once and the verb/verb phrase twice. Label any direct object-D.O.

Remember: To set, to raise, and to lay (lays, laid, laying) will have a direct object.

1.   The portable telephone is (lying, laying) by the television.

2.   That student (rises, raises) his hand constantly.

3.   Jonah (sits, sets) in the back pew at church.

4.   Do you (sit, set) an alarm clock at bedtime?

G.   Directions: List the 20 linking verbs. _____

_____

H.   Directions: Cross out any prepositional phrase(s). Underline the subject once and the verb twice. Write A if the verb is action; write L if the verb is linking.

Remember: A linking verb can be replaced by a form of to be: is, am, are, was, or were.

1. _____   These chips taste terrible.

2. _____   A guest tasted the dip with a finger.

3. _____   The family remained calm during the fire.

4. _____   A customer felt the texture of the tweed suit.

168

Name_____

Date_____

I. Directions: Write the contraction.

1. they are - _____   5. there is - _____

2. does not - _____   6. will not - _____

3. I am - _____   7. she is - _____

4. we have - _____   8. would not - _____

J. Directions: Cross out any prepositional phrase(s). Underline the subject once
    and the verb/verb phrase twice. Determine the tense and write
    present, *past*, or *future* in the space provided.

1. _____   Shelby lives in Montana.

2. _____   I shall send you some money.

3. _____   The toddler swam to the side of the pool.

4. _____   Bo and he dive for oysters.

5. _____   Will you have a garage sale soon?

K. Directions: Write intj. above any interjection.

1. Yippee! We're moving at last!

2. You forgot the tickets again! Oh no!

L. Directions: Write conj. above any conjunction.

1. The front door or the back one needs to be oiled.

2. We ordered pizza and cola, but it arrived too late.

M. Directions: Write <u>A</u> if the word is abstract; write <u>C</u> if it is concrete.

1. _____   love   3. _____   scissors   5. _____   hope

2. _____   applesauce   4. _____   water   6. _____   fountain

Name_____

Date_____

N. Directions: Write <u>C</u> if the noun is common; write <u>P</u> if it is proper.

1. _____ PERSON   3. _____ FOOD   5. _____ CANADA

2. _____ JOHN ADAMS   4. _____ GOAT   6. _____ COUNTRY

O. Directions: Write <u>A</u> if the underlined word serves as an adjective; write <u>N</u> if the underlined word serves as a noun.

1. _____   The catcher threw the <u>baseball</u> to second base.

2. _____   She grasped the <u>baseball</u> bat very tightly.

3. _____   This <u>trash</u> can is full.

4. _____   Will <u>trash</u> be picked up soon?

P. Directions: Write <u>V</u> if the underlined word serves as a verb; write <u>N</u> if the underlined word serves as a noun.

1. _____   In tense situations, she <u>handles</u> herself well.

2. _____   Several <u>handles</u> on the chest are broken.

3. _____   Those boys often <u>fall</u> around to be funny.

4. _____   Leaves change colors in the <u>fall</u>.

Q. Directions: Write the possessive form.

1. a jump rope belonging to Lisa - _____

2. shoes belonging to Mrs. Jones - _____

3. luggage belonging to travelers - _____

4. toys belonging to children - _____

5. tools belonging to one man - _____

170

R. Directions: Write the plural of the noun.

1. fence - _____   5. eyelash - _____

2. mass - _____   6. delay - _____

3. calf - _____   7. poem - _____

4. story - _____   8. punch - _____

S. Directions: Box any nouns. (Determining adjectives will help you find many nouns.)

1. A single rose bloomed on the bush.

2. Two deer and an enormous squirrel live in that forest.

3. Some papers and several booklets are in his briefcase.

4. Grandma's house has yellow siding and a brown roof.

5. Their science professor is a small man with large glasses.

6. A lawyer talked with three jurists on the third floor of the courthouse.

T. Directions: Cross out any prepositional phrase(s). Underline the subject once and the verb/verb phrase twice.   Label any predicate nominative-P.N. Then, write the proof on the line provided.

1. The winners of the badminton game were Hope and Cecil.

Proof: _____

2. Mrs. Tarbell is the mother of those four children.

Proof: _____

3. Their favorite national park is Yellowstone.

Proof: _____

ADVERBS

Adverbs are words that tell <u>how</u>, <u>when</u>, <u>where</u>, and <u>to what extent</u>. They modify verbs, adjectives, and other adverbs.

How:

Some adverbs tell **how**. These usually modify verbs. They often end in **ly**.

> Example: <u>Tracy talks</u> quickly.　　(*Quickly* tells **how** Tracy talks.)
>
> <u>Tracy runs</u> fast.　　(*Fast* tells **how** Tracy runs.)

<u>ADVERB OR ADJECTIVE</u>:

	Adjective	**Adverb** (telling how someone does something)
Examples:	careful (person)	carefully
	happy	happily
	slow	slowly
	fast	fast (Some do not change.)

Name_____

Date_____

A. Directions: Write the adverb. Use a dictionary if necessary.

ADJECTIVE   **ADVERB**

1.   easy   _____

2.   smooth   _____

3.   fine   _____

4.   careless   _____

5.   peaceful   _____

6.   beautiful   _____

7.   slow   _____

8.   patient   _____

B. Directions: Select the correct word:

1. That neighbor is a (kind, kindly) woman.

2. She speaks (kind, kindly) to us.

3. That man is very (hungry, hungrily).

4. That man ate his meal (hungry, hungrily).

5. He spoke (angry, angrily).

6. The (angry, angrily) child refused the lollipop.

7. Senator Harving speaks (loud, loudly).

8. Senator Harving has a (loud, loudly) voice.

9. The (merry, merrily) children climbed the slide.

10. The children slid down the slide (merry, merrily) during the afternoon recess.

178

A. Directions: Write the adverb. Use a dictionary if necessary.

ADJECTIVE	**ADVERB**
1. loving	_____
2. weird	_____
3. fast	_____
4. helpless	_____
5. faithful	_____
6. timid	_____
7. dangerous	_____
8. lucky	_____

B. Directions: Select the correct word:

1. Jay hits the ball (powerful, powerfully) to the outfield.

2. Jay is a (powerful, powerfully) hitter.

3. The judge can be very (stern, sternly) to witnesses.

4. The judge spoke (stern, sternly) to the witness.

5. The (demanding, demandingly) child grabbed the candy and ran.

6. A child who grabs candy acts (demanding, demandingly).

7. The woman looked (sad, sadly) at the telephone bill.

8. The (sad, sadly) woman doesn't know how she will pay her telephone bill.

9. The (joyful, joyfully) participants awaited for the winners' names to be announced.

10. They jumped up (joyfully, joyful) when their names were called.

Name_____   **ADVERBS**
                                              How?

Date_____

Directions: Cross out any prepositional phrase(s). Underline the subject once and
              the verb/verb phrase twice. Label any adverb (<u>ADV.</u>) that tells **HOW**.
              In the space provided, explain the use of the adverb in the sentence.

                                    ADV.
              Example: A <u>roadrunner</u> <u>goes</u> quickly ~~across open highways~~.

                          <u>   Quickly tells HOW a roadrunner goes.   </u>

1. A new employee listened carefully to the directions.

    _____

2. The college students walked slowly to class.

    _____

3. Fans cheer enthusiastically for their team.

    _____

4. The child peeped timidly around the corner.

    _____

5. A truck was weaving dangerously through heavy traffic.

    _____

6. Their mom cries softly during some movies.

    _____

7. The train whistle blew loudly.

    _____

8. A racquetball player hit the ball hard against the wall.

    _____

Name_____   **ADVERBS**
                               How?

Date_____

Directions: Cross out any prepositional phrase(s). Underline the subject once and
the verb/verb phrase twice. Label any adverb (ADV.) that tells **HOW**.
In the space provided, explain the use of the adverb in the sentence.

                                   ADV.
Example: The <u>athlete</u> <u><u>wheezed</u></u> mildly ~~after the event~~.

               <u>Mildly tells HOW the athlete wheezed.</u>

1.   A jet zoomed fast toward the ocean.

     _____

2.   A deer lay silently near a tree.

     _____

3.   Birds chirped noisily in a flowering bush.

     _____

4.   Each morning, she stretches lazily by her bed.

     _____

5.   His dog lay quietly under his desk.

     _____

6.   Bicycle riders pulled their bikes cautiously to the curb.

     _____

7.   Cheerfully, she pumped gas at the local garage.

     _____

8.   The animal with the hurt leg whined softly.

     _____

Name_____   **ADVERBS**
                                          How?

Date_____

Directions: Cross out any prepositional phrase(s). Underline the subject once and
              the verb/verb phrase twice. Label any adverb (ADV.) that tells **HOW**.
              In the space provided, explain the use of the adverb in the sentence.

                              ADV.
              Example: The wind blows gently ~~through that canyon~~.

                      _____Gently tells HOW the wind blows._____

1. The child stomped his foot angrily.

    _____

2. Abruptly, the car stopped at the intersection.

    _____

3. After his bath, Fido shook himself briskly.

    _____

4. Her corsage slowly wilted during the dance.

    _____

5. The travelers ate hungrily at the Wayside Inn.

    _____

6. That truck turns corners sharply.

    _____

7. The teenage girl spoke harshly to her brother with the squirt gun.

    _____

8. A child in the airport laid his head sleepily on the back of a chair.

    _____

ADVERBS
Good or Well?

Good is an adjective.
Good will describe a noun or a pronoun.

> Examples: He is a **good** high jumper.
>
> That last show was a **good** one.
>
> These cookies are **good**.

Remember: A linking verb such as *to feel, to taste, to look, to become,* or *to seem* will use **good**.

> First, determine if the verb is linking by inserting *is, am, are, was,* or *were* above it. If the sentence makes sense, use <u>good</u> instead of <u>well</u>.

> **is**
> Examples: This <u>soup</u> <u>tastes</u> **good**.   ____<u>good soup</u>____
> **was**
> The <u>jockey</u> <u>became</u> **good** ~~at riding~~.   ____<u>good jockey</u>____

The forms for comparing **good**: good, better (2), and best (3 or more).
>   That baby is a **good** sleeper.
>   This baby is a **better** sleeper than his sister. (2)
>   He is the **best** sleeper in the entire church nursery. (3 or more)

Well is an adverb.
Well tells how and modifies the verb.
Anytime someone tells how they performed an *ACTION*, **well** is used.

> Examples: He <u>speaks</u> **well**.
>
> The clerk <u>operates</u> the cash register **well**.
>
> <u>Has</u> he <u>done</u> his job **well**?

Exception: Use **well** to signify one's physical condition.
>   Example: I don't feel **well**.

The forms for comparing **well**: well, better (2), and best (3 or more)
>   She swims **well**.
>   Joan's sister swims **better** than she does. (2)
>   Blake swims **best** of all the boys in his 4-H club.

Directions: Write **good** or **well** in the space provided.

1. You are a _____ singer.

    You sing _____.

2. Amanda flies _____.

    Amanda is a _____ pilot.

3. Councilman Jackson speaks _____.

    Councilman Jackson is a _____ speaker.

4. Aunt Edna and Uncle Frank are _____ cooks.

    Aunt Edna and Uncle Frank cook _____.

5. Scooter is a _____ catcher.

    Scooter catches _____.

6. Grandma Moses painted _____.

    Grandma Moses was a _____ artist.

7. That lady sews _____.

    That lady is a _____ seamstress.

8. The maid is a _____ cleaner.

    The maid cleans _____.

184

Name_____

Date_____

Directions: Write **good** or **well** in the space provided.

1.   She washes her car _____.

2.   Nan is a _____ shoe shiner.

3.   I don't feel _____.

4.   His teacher writes _____.

5.   Please be a _____ listener.

6.   Her mom plays baseball _____.

7.   The gardener trimmed the bushes _____ last week.

8.   Mr. Howell is a _____ chiropractor.

9.   You did so _____.

10.   That cowboy is a _____ rancher.

11.   A _____ babysitter is important.

12.   Harvey doesn't pack a suitcase too _____.

13.   The boys threw the balls _____ and won purple stuffed animals.

14.   Frances Ann, a member of the swimming team, swims very _____.

15.   The kindergartner says her *ABC's* _____.

Name_____

Date_____

Directions: Write **good** or **well** in the space provided.

1. A road construction crew cleaned up _____ after the storm.

2. Sometimes a newborn baby doesn't sleep _____.

3. You have done a _____ job with that.

4. Martha doesn't feel _____ tonight.

5. This pencil has not been sharpened _____.

6. Lori and Dawn are _____ volleyball players.

7. Fasten this gate _____ for security.

8. The spaghetti and garlic bread taste _____.

9. Carmen is _____ at making dolls.

10. Your shoelaces aren't tied _____.

11. Did your parents tell you to wash your face _____ in the morning?

12. We had a _____ time at the party.

13. Have you done _____ on the test?

14. His condition remained _____ after surgery.

15. Olivia needs a _____ job with enough money to pay the rent.

ADVERBS

Where

Some adverbs tell **where.**

An adverb that tells <u>where</u> usually modifies (goes over to) a verb.

Some adverbs that tell <u>where</u>:

here	in*	inside
there	out	outside
somewhere	up	around
everywhere	down	upstream
nowhere	uptown	far
where	downtown	nearby

🍓🍓🍓🍓🍓🍓🍓🍓🍓🍓🍓🍓🍓🍓🍓🍓🍓🍓🍓🍓🍓🍓🍓🍓🍓🍓🍓🍓🍓🍓🍓🍓🍓🍓🍓

Some adverbs that tell **<u>where</u>** were learned originally as prepositions.

Example: The <u>boy</u> <u>rolled</u> ~~down the hill~~.   (preposition)

The <u>boy</u> <u>fell</u> **down** ~~on the wet floor~~.   (adverb telling where)

A boat <u>driver</u> <u>leaned</u> **over** and <u>whispered</u> to a passenger. (adverb)

That athlete jumps ~~over hurdles~~ well. (preposition)

🍓🍓🍓🍓🍓🍓🍓🍓🍓🍓🍓🍓🍓🍓🍓🍓🍓🍓🍓🍓🍓🍓🍓🍓🍓🍓🍓🍓🍓🍓🍓🍓🍓🍓🍓

Steps in determining adverbs that tell <u>where</u>:

1. Cross out any prepositional phrases. Adverbs telling <u>where</u> will not be in a prepositional phrase.
2. Underline the subject once and the verb/verb phrase twice.
3. Look for any word that tells <u>where</u>.

Name_____

Date_____

Directions: Cross out any prepositional phrase(s). Underline the subject once and the verb/verb phrase twice. Label any adverb (ADV.) that tells **WHERE**. In the space provided, explain the use of the adverb in the sentence.

                                    ADV.
Example: I took my form over ~~to that nurse~~ ~~with the white hat~~.

_____Over tells WHERE I took my form._____

1. Jerry fell down on his scooter.

   _____

2. Ellen is coming here in the morning.

   _____

3. We have searched everywhere for the lost puppy.

   _____

4. The astronomer looked up into the telescope.

   _____

5. Would you like to sit there by the window?

   _____

6. Our raft had floated far into the bay.

   _____

7. A security guard looked around in the hotel.

   _____

8. They played inside on a rainy day.

   _____

Name_____   **ADVERBS**
                                                Where?
Date_____

Directions: Cross out any prepositional phrase(s). Underline the subject once and
              the verb/verb phrase twice. Label any adverb (ADV.) that tells **WHERE**.
              In the space provided, explain the use of the adverb in the sentence.

                                ADV.
        Example: She pointed westward ~~toward the setting sun~~.

                   ___Westward tells WHERE she pointed.___

1.   They must have gone somewhere.

     _____

2.   A passenger came aboard.

     _____

3.   Where are you going?

     _____

4.   The sports club members waded upstream to fish.

     _____

5.   I can't find my books anywhere.

     _____

6.   Do you live nearby?

     _____

7.   That freeway goes downtown to the business section.

     _____

8.   Do not come in without your shoes.

     _____

Name_____   **ADVERBS**
                                          Where?

Date_____

Directions: Cross out any prepositional phrase(s). Underline the subject once and
              the verb/verb phrase twice. Label any adverb (ADV.) that tells **WHERE**.
              In the space provided, explain the use of the adverb in the sentence.

                              ADV.
       Example: The <u>couple</u> <u>lives</u> farther ~~down the winding road~~.

                    _____Farther tells WHERE the couple lives._____

1.   I should have stayed home.

     _____

2.   A gull glided downward over the ocean.

     _____

3.   His hat fell off into the water.

     _____

4.   You may sit here by the window.

     _____

5.   This hallway in the Winchester House goes nowhere.

     _____

6.   There are no dolphins in this area.

     _____

7.   A man in his late twenties skipped out of the library with an armload of books.

     _____

8.   She approached the finish line and dashed across to victory.

     _____

190

ADVERBS

When?

Some adverbs tell **when.**

An adverb that tells **when** usually modifies (or goes over to) the verb/verb phrase.   It will be only one word.

Examples: Yesterday <u>he went</u> home.   (*Yesterday* tells when he went.)

<u>I shall buy</u> a gift ~~for you~~ later. (*Later* tells when I shall buy a gift.)

Some words that tell **when** are:

tonight	soon	ever	nightly
today	sooner	never	daily
now	when	forever	hourly
late	always	whenever	early
later	yet	then	afterwards

Steps to determine adverbs that tell **when.**

1.   Cross out any prepositional phrase(s).

2.   Underline the subject once and the verb/verb phrase twice.

3.   Look for any word that tells <u>when</u>.

                         ADV.
Example: The <u>nurse</u> immediately <u>rushed</u> ~~to the patient's room~~.

Name_____

Date_____

Directions: Cross out any prepositional phrase(s). Underline the subject once and
the verb/verb phrase twice. Label any adverb (<u>ADV.</u>) that tells **WHEN**.
In the space provided, explain the use of the adverb in the sentence.

ADV.
Example: <u>They</u> always <u>brush</u> their teeth ~~in the morning~~.

_____Always tells WHEN they brush their teeth._____

1. Suddenly, the truck swerved off the road.

_____

2. Tonight, I shall read for a few hours.

_____

3. She never leaves for work before nine o'clock.

_____

4. The gentleman frequently feeds the pigeons in the park.

_____

5. Their family goes to church regularly.

_____

6. A physical exam was recommended yesterday.

_____

7. That store operates daily.

_____

8. They often surf in the afternoon.

_____

Name_____   **ADVERBS**
                                  When?
Date_____

Directions: Cross out any prepositional phrase(s). Underline the subject once and
              the verb/verb phrase twice. Label any adverb (ADV.) that tells **WHEN**.
              In the space provided, explain the use of the adverb in the sentence.

                                ADV.
              Example: Will this rain last forever?

                 _____Forever tells WHEN this rain will last._____

1.   You always seem happy.

     _____

2.   Martin goes to Oregon yearly.

     _____

3.   Someday, you must visit Heard Museum.

     _____

4.   When will he be finished?

     _____

5.   The toddler seldom takes a nap.

     _____

6.   Mom and Dad usually donate used clothes to charity.

     _____

7.   The children take baths nightly.

     _____

8.   I shall go with you later.

     _____

Name_____   **ADVERBS**
                                            When?

Date_____

Directions: Cross out any prepositional phrase(s). Underline the subject once and
              the verb/verb phrase twice. Label any adverb (ADV.) that tells **WHEN**.
              In the space provided, explain the use of the adverb in the sentence.

                                    ADV.
       Example: Is Santa coming soon?

                        _____Soon tells WHEN Santa is coming._____

1. They left the fast food restaurant suddenly.

    _____

2. Kevin burned the cookies again.

    _____

3. Please do that now.

    _____

4. Duane recently moved to San Diego.

    _____

5. We enjoy a circus now and then.

    _____

6. She pulled weeds immediately after lunch.

    _____

7. Sooner or later, Dad must make a decision about the job.

    _____

8. Susan will save her money now and buy a home soon.

    _____

194

ADVERBS

To What Extent?

Some adverbs tell to what extent.

There are seven common adverbs that tell to what extent: <u>not</u>, <u>so</u>, <u>very</u>, <u>too</u>, <u>quite</u>, <u>rather</u>, <u>somewhat</u>.

There are other adverbs that tell **to what extent** (extremely, unusually).

These adverbs can modify (go over to) a **verb**, an **adjective**, or another **adverb**:

VERB

Examples: I <u>would</u> **rather** <u>stay</u> here.   (Rather tells **to what extent** I would stay.)

ADJ.

This is a **very** pretty picture. (Very tells **to what extent** pretty.)

ADV.

Don't walk **so** slowly. (So tells **to what extent** slowly.)

🍓🍓🍓🍓🍓🍓🍓🍓🍓🍓🍓🍓🍓🍓🍓🍓🍓🍓🍓🍓🍓🍓🍓🍓🍓🍓🍓🍓🍓🍓🍓🍓🍓🍓🍓

Occasionally, an adverb that tells *to what extent* will occur within a prepositional phrase. Hence, the following steps need to be taken in determining these adverbs.

1. First, delete prepositional phrases. Check each prepositional phrase to see if an adverb telling <u>to what extent</u> is in it.

   ADV.

   Example: The door ~~by the bedroom~~ did not open ~~onto a~~ very ~~large patio~~.

2. Underline the subject once and the verb/verb phrase twice.

   ADV.

   Example: The <u>door</u> ~~by the bedroom~~ <u>did</u> not <u>open</u> ~~onto a~~ very ~~large patio~~.

3. Look for any other adverbs in the sentence that tell *to what extent*.

   ADV.   ADV.

   Example: The <u>door</u> ~~by the bedroom~~ <u>did</u> not <u>open</u> ~~onto a~~ very ~~large patio~~.

195

There are seven adverbs that commonly tell *to what extent.* These are **not (n't)**, **so**, **very**, **too**, **quite**, **rather**, and **somewhat**. Although there are others, these seven appear repeatedly and tell *to what extent.* (Others may include *completely, extremely,* or *unusually.*) Be sure to memorize **not (n't)**, **so**, **very**, **too**, **quite**, **rather**, and **somewhat**.

Directions: Circle any adverb(s) telling *to what extent*.

1. You look so sad.

2. The parents were very upset.

3. Those painters are too busy to come today.

4. Do not waste your time with that.

5. He is a rather calm jockey.

6. Debra is quite happy to sit and knit.

7. Don't become so fearful.

8. Mr. and Mrs. Little are rather concerned about the concert.

9. The boat left the harbor very suddenly.

10. He looks at me rather strangely.

11. Sydney is completely interested in the deal.

12. The child appears extremely sleepy.

13. We felt somewhat ill after eating the salad.

14. You are too worried about driving to Tulsa.

15. Do not spend so much time in the bathroom.

Name_____   **ADVERBS**
                                         To What Extent?
Date_____

There are seven adverbs that commonly tell *to what extent*. These are **not (n't)**, **so**, **very**, **too**, **quite**, **rather**, and **somewhat**. Although there are others, these appear repeatedly and tell *to what extent*. (Others may include *completely, extremely,* or *unusually.*) Be sure to memorize the seven commonly used adverbs.

Directions: Circle any adverb(s) telling *to what extent*.

1.   These clothes are too worn out to sell.

2.   Mrs. Hand is so excited about skydiving.

3.   Her friend is somewhat timid.

4.   That forest is rather beautiful.

5.   This doughnut is too sticky.

6.   A glass of lemonade can be very refreshing.

7.   The somewhat burned egg was scraped from the pan.

8.   This telephone is extremely old.

9.   A radio is playing too loudly for me.

10.   I would not like to go there this summer.

11.   His answer was not very clear.

12.   Her sister is unusually tall.

13.   He is somewhat shy, but his brother is rather outgoing.

14.   Jenny seems quite perturbed by John's rather funny remark.

15.   Don't give up so easily.

Name_____

Date_____

Directions: Label **any** adverb(s) in each sentence.

Remember: Adverbs tell **HOW, WHEN, WHERE, AND TO WHAT EXTENT**.

Suggestion: Cross out any prepositional phrase(s). However, check to see if one of the 7 adverbs that tell *to what extent* may be in any prepositional phrase. If it is, label that adverb. Underline the subject once and the verb/verb phrase twice. Next, go through the sentence looking specifically for any adverbs that tell **how**. Reread the sentence, searching for any adverbs that tell **when**. Next, look for any adverbs that tell **where**. Finally, look for any adverbs that tell **to what extent** and are not located in a prepositional phrase. This process may sound long, but once you do it step-by-step, it will become fast and will help you to determine adverbs.

                    ADV.   ADV.   ADV.
Example: Yesterday, a <u>man</u> ~~with a very lovely wife~~ <u><u>snorkled</u></u> here.

1.   That customer comes in daily.

2.   Her mother in South Dakota will not visit soon.

3.   Monica stayed there alone.

4.   Those children play nicely together.

5.   Dr. Hubbard often seems very tired.

6.   Later, some citizens wrote rather long letters to their senator.

7.   Afterwards, the family went up into an observation tower.

8.   At the family gathering, they sat everywhere on the lawn and chatted about their

      somewhat unusual pets.

Directions: Label **any** adverb(s) in each sentence.

Remember: Adverbs tell **HOW, WHEN, WHERE,** AND **TO WHAT EXTENT**.

Suggestion: Cross out any prepositional phrase(s). However, check to see if one of the 7 adverbs that tell *to what extent* may be in any prepositional phrase. If it is, label that adverb. Underline the subject once and the verb/verb phrase twice. Next, go through the sentence looking specifically for any adverbs that tell **how**. Reread the sentence, searching for any adverbs that tell **when**. Next, look for any adverbs that tell **where**. Finally, look for any adverbs that tell **to what extent** and are not located in a prepositional phrase. This process may sound long, but once you do it step-by-step, it will become fast and will help you to determine adverbs.

                          ADV. ADV.
Example: Their <u>coach</u> <u><u>sat</u></u> there silently ~~with his head in his hands~~.

1. Yesterday, clouds rolled in from the west.

2. He reacted so strangely to the news.

3. The bride smiled down at her somewhat frightened flower girl.

4. Very heavy rains rapidly flooded the area.

5. You may sit somewhere nearby.

6. There are not any snakes in the Dayhoff's pond now.

7. The bathroom has been cleaned too hurriedly.

8. Their uncle always travels everywhere during his summer vacation.

ADVERBS

Degrees of Adverbs

Adverbs often make comparisons:

The **comparative** form compares two things.

The **superlative** form compares three things or more.

comparative: The first batter hit the ball **harder** than the second one.
(Two are being compared for how the ball was hit.)

superlative: Cameron hit the ball **hardest** during the game.
(A comparison with Cameron and everyone else who hit the ball during the game is being made.)

There are three ways to form the comparative and the superlative:

A. **Comparative** - comparing <u>2</u>:

1. Add **er** to most one-syllable adverbs:

   hard/harder   fast/faster

2. Place **more** before most two or more syllable adverbs:

   gently/more gently   recently/more recently

3. Some adverbs totally change form:

   badly/worse   well/better

B. **Superlative** - comparing <u>3</u> or more:

1. Add <u>**est**</u> to most one-syllable adverbs:

   hard/hardest   fast/fastest

2. Place <u>**most**</u> before most two or more syllable adverbs:

   gently/most gently   recently/most recently

3. Some adverbs totally change form:

   badly/worst   well/best

Adverb	Comparative	Superlative
well	better	best
lazily	more lazily	most lazily
hurriedly	more hurriedly	most hurriedly
sleepily	more sleepily	most sleepily

*<u>Less</u> for the comparative and <u>least</u> for the superlative may also be used.

Name_____

Date_____

Directions: An adjective form has been given. Write the adverb form in the first blank.
Then, write the comparative form in B and the superlative form in C.

Examples: Margo did her work _____rapidly_____ (rapid).
However, Kent does his work _____more rapidly_____ than Margo.
Of all the office workers, Helen does her work __most rapidly__ .

1. A. Penny walks _____ (slow).

   B. Her brother walks _____ .

   C. Of the entire family, their dad walks _____ .

2. A. An acrobat flipped _____ (smooth).

   B. This acrobat flips _____ than his partner.

   C. That acrobat flips _____ during her third act.

3. A. I spoke _____ (kind) to the new neighbor.

   B. Roberto speaks _____ to his friends than Kurt.

   C. Of all the girls on the cheering squad, Franny speaks _____ .

4. A. The cafeteria server works _____ (careful).

   B. Of the two gardeners, the tall one works _____ .

   C. You worked hard on the three assignments, but you did the first one _____

   _____ .

5. A. The athlete standing by the coach runs _____ (fast).

   B. However, the one getting a drink runs _____ .

   C. The athlete without his helmet runs _____ of the whole team.

202

Directions: An adjective form has been given. Write the adverb form in the first blank.
Then, write the comparative form in B and the superlative form in C.

Examples: Carlo sits _____restlessly_____ (restless).
He sits even ____more restlessly_____ than his little brother.
His older brother sits _____most restlessly_____ of the family.

1. A.   She does that _____ (easy).

  B.   Lauren does the trick _____ than I.

  C.   Of the triplets, Dee Dee does the trick _____.

2. A.   Heyward hits the ball _____ (hard).

  B.   His younger son hits it _____ than Heyward.

  C.   However, his oldest son hits it _____ of the entire family.

3. A.   Joel moved _____ (recent).

  B.   Tammi moved _____ than her friend.

  C.   Of all their travels, the Clarks enjoyed the trip taken _____.

4. A.   A visitor stepped onto the ladder bridge _____ (hesitant).

  B.   Brad climbed on the horse _____ than his sister did.

  C.   He jumps _____ of their skydiving team.

5. A.   Don't answer so _____ (sharp).

  B.   This fire bell rings _____ than the old one.

  C.   The parent answered _____ the third time he said no.

Name_____

Date_____

Directions: Select the correct adverb form.

Example: Ron walks (**more slowly**, most slowly) than his teammate.

1. Jacob answered (more quickly, most quickly) than his friend.

2. He fell down (harder, hardest) the second time he fell.

3. The student reciting a speech spoke (more confidently, most confidently) during the third practice.

4. In that family, the oldest speaks (more softly, most softly).

5. That patient went home (earlier, more early) than his roommate.

6. The carpet layer takes breaks (more often, oftener) than his helper.

7. That raccoon climbed the tree (faster, fastest) of all the animals.

8. Morning storms seem to occur (more suddenly, most suddenly) than afternoon ones.

9. This last check in the checkbook has been written (more legibly, most legibly).

10. Bean plants grow (taller, tallest) than corn in their garden.

11. The customer behaved (more rudely, most rudely) the second time she explained the problem to the clerk.

12. The boys and girls played (more roughly, most roughly) during the third game.

13. That volcano erupted (more violently, most violently) the second time.

14. Of all the gifts, she likes her tennis shoes (better, best).

15. In the round of golf, she hit the ball (more swiftly, most swiftly) at hole four.

Directions: Select the correct adverb form.

   Example: The actress reacted (**more tearfully**, most tearfully) the second time.

1.   The little girl plays (more quietly, most quietly) than her older sister.

2.   The teenager did (worse, worst) on the second driving test.

3.   A black kitten chased the ball (more playfully, most playfully) than the white one.

4.   He shook the third rug (more furiously, most furiously).

5.   The wind blew (more strongly, most strongly) during the second storm.

6.   That girl smiles (more brightly, most brightly) of the three models.

7.   A large kite soared (higher, highest) than the smaller one.

8.   This ballet dancer moves (more gracefully, most gracefully) of all the performers.

9.   The runners cut the corner (more sharply, most sharply) during the third try.

10.   This new canoe glides (more slowly, most slowly) than the old one.

11.   At the party, they arrived (sooner, soonest) than the Smith family.

12.   Dick sleds (more frequently, most frequently) than he toboggans.

13.   The model smiled (more brightly, most brightly) for the fifth commercial.

14.   I feel (badly, worse) today than I did yesterday.

15.   That driver stopped his car (more recklessly, most recklessly) at the second traffic light than at the first one.

ADVERBS
Double Negatives

Negative words include: no, not (n't), never, none, no one, nobody, nothing, nowhere, scarcely, hardly.
Don't use two negatives in a sentence.

Examples: **WRONG:**   I don't want nothing.

   RIGHT: I don't want anything.
   OR
   I want nothing.

   WRONG: She won't give nobody money.

   RIGHT: She won't give anybody money.
   OR
   She will give nobody money.

   WRONG: I hardly get no time to myself.

   RIGHT: I hardly get any time to myself.
   OR
   I get no time to myself.

••

Neither is also a negative word and should not be used with another negative.

   Examples: **WRONG:** Neither wants to go nowhere.
   RIGHT: Neither wants to go anywhere.

Neither may be used with *nor*:   Neither Mother nor her friends are bowling today.
••

It is acceptable to use *no* as a response at the beginning of a sentence and then use another negative word after it.
   Example: **No**, I do **not** want a cookie.

206

A. Directions: Select the correct word.

1. He never leaves me (any, no) money.

2. This isn't (anybody's, nobody's) business.

3. He (can, can't) hardly hear you.

4. I can't find a quarter (nowhere, anywhere).

5. We have not eaten (no, any) potatoes.

6. She doesn't want (nothing, anything) to drink.

7. You're not allowed to go (nowhere, anywhere) alone.

8. The man didn't have (no, any) trouble fixing his car.

9. They never do (anything, nothing).

10. I don't want (none, any).

B. Each sentence contains double negatives. Rewrite each sentence correctly.

1. She doesn't want none.   _____

2. I never want nothing.   _____

3. They scarcely go nowhere.   _____

4. Nobody wants none.   _____

5. Don't go with no one.   _____

Name_____

Date_____

A. Directions: Select the correct word.

1. The soda fountain doesn't have (no, any) chairs.

2. I hadn't (ever, never) seen that.

3. That store scarcely has (no, any) products.

4. Nobody wants to go (anywhere, nowhere).

5. Don't do that (never, ever) again.

6. He hardly earned (anything, nothing) last summer.

7. No one ever wants (any, none).

8. You aren't supposed to do (nobody's, anybody's) work.

9. This lawn mower (has, hasn't) hardly been used.

10. Don't drink (no, any) water from the creek.

B. Each sentence contains double negatives. Rewrite each sentence correctly.

1. He's not mad at nobody. _____

2. His mother doesn't want
    nothing. _____

3. Don't try that never again. _____

4. This computer doesn't have
    no keyboard. _____

5. There isn't hardly any
    time to do that. _____

208

Directions: Choose **any** adverb(s) in each sentence.

                    ADV.   ADV.   ADV.
Example: We <u>can go</u> **there later** for a **very** brief workout.

1.   Her hair is very curly today.

2.   Those sand dunes are quite steep for me to steer easily.

3.   Abruptly, she stood up and yelled with too much anger in her voice.

4.   The welder carefully placed two pieces of steel sideways.

5.   Several very large tumbleweeds twirled fiercely around in the air.

6.   That deli owner does not cut his pickles lengthwise.

7.   When has Mrs. Stanford gone somewhere without her children?

8.   Tomorrow, don't go outside until lunch.

Directions: Select the correct answer.

1.   This new machine works (more steadily, most steadily) than the old one.

2.   Anita climbs the tree (more easily, most easily) of the four girls.

3.   Did you arrive (later, latest) than Miss Calhoun?

4.   The third car stopped (suddener, most suddenly).

Directions: Select the correct answer.

1.   He never goes (anywhere, nowhere) without his hat.

2.   Nobody wants (none, any) right now.

3.   She hardly has (no, any) money.

Name_____   **CUMULATIVE REVIEW**

Date_____

A. Directions: Cross out any prepositional phrase(s). Underline the subject once
    and the verb/verb phrase twice.

1. One of the birds flew among the branches.

2. A lizard had crawled under a rock in the garden.

3. After the beginning of the third quarter, the snack bar was closed.

4. Please move the boxes toward the middle of the garage.

****

B. Directions: Write the contraction.

1. will not - _____   3. has not - _____

2. we have - _____   4. we are - _____
****

C. Directions: Write the tense in the blank provided.

1. _____ The council will meet to discuss the plans.

2. _____ Those Native Americans weave beautiful baskets.

3. _____ The mason laid bricks for the patio.
****

D. Write intj. above any interjection and conj. above any conjunction.

1. The janitor pushed the door open and propped it with a broom.

2. Good grief! The pen has leaked all over my shirt!
****

E. Write A if the noun is abstract; write C if the noun is concrete.

1. ____ butterfly   2. ____ patience   3. ____ anger   4. ____ air
****

F. Directions: Write C if the noun is common; write P if it is proper.

1. ___ LAKE ERIE   2. ___ BELL   3. ___ BUILDING   4. ___ SEARS TOWER
210

G.   Directions: Write **N** if the underlined word is a noun.   Write **A** if the underlined
                word is an adjective.   Write **V** if the underlined word is a verb.

1. _____ The elderly ladies go for a <u>walk</u> every day.

2. _____ The first four pupils will <u>walk</u> to the end of the line.

3. _____ A <u>cat</u> dish has been placed by the door.

4. _____ The Simpson family has been given a <u>cat</u>.
****

H.   Directions: Write the possessive form.

1.   clothes belonging to a man - _____

2.   a ball belonging to Chris - _____

3.   a hole belonging to mice - _____

4.   popsicles belonging to girls - _____
****

I.   Directions: Write the plural.

1.   lash - _____   2. bug - _____   3. child - _____
4.   box - _____   5. list - _____   6. lens- _____
****

J.   Directions: Box any nouns:

1.   Several lights have been broken near that alley.
2.   His bike has a loose seat.
3.   Jolene's dad is having a party for some friends.
****

K.   Directions: Write **D.O.** if the underlined word is a direct object, **P.N.** if the
                underlined word is a predicate nominative, and **P.A.** if the underlined
                word is a predicate adjective.

1.   _____ The child threw a <u>ball</u> to his friend.

2.   _____ The winner is <u>Juan</u>.

3.   _____ This bread tastes <u>stale</u>.

SENTENCE TYPES

The four types of sentences are declarative, interrogative, imperative, and exclamatory.

1. A **declarative** sentence makes a **statement**.
    A declarative sentence ends in a period.

    Examples: Spain and Portugal are on the same peninsula.

    Roberta eats ketchup on crackers.

2. An **interrogative** sentence asks a **question**.
    An interrogative sentence ends in a question mark.

    Examples: How many taste buds does a human have?

    Are there any bees in that hive?

3. An **imperative** sentence gives a **command**.
    An imperative sentence ends in a period.

    Examples: Pass the salt, please.

    Take this home with you.

4. An **exclamatory** sentence shows **emotion**.
    An exclamatory sentence ends with an exclamation point.

    Examples: The water is flooding the kitchen!

    Yuck!   You threw that on the floor!

∞∞

An entire interrogative sentence will ask a quesition.

Example: Can you fix the car?

A sentence will be declarative if part of the sentence implies a question.

Example: Mr. Hanes asked the mechanic if he could fix the car.

Directions: Write the sentence type on the line.

1. _____ Groceries were purchased early in the
                             morning.

2. _____ Is a dove a sign of peace?

3. _____ You're here!

4. _____ Please read this.

5. _____ A peacock displays his feathers.

6. _____ Yeah! We're finished!

7. _____ Cabbage is a very healthy vegetable.

8. _____ Put your papers in this trash.

9. _____ What game are they playing?

10. _____ Jane asked if she could go.

11. _____ We've lost the gas cap.

12. _____ May we watch television for an hour?

Name_____

Date_____

Directions: Write the sentence type on the line.

1. _____ Bee hives are very clean.

2. _____ Have you ever eaten kale?

3. _____ Grab the fire extinguisher.

4. _____ We won!

5. _____ Stop at the red line.

6. _____ They listen well.

7. _____ Would you like a hot dog?

8. _____ Clean your room.

9. _____ The closet was cleaned once a year.

10. _____ Have you finished your homework?

11. _____ Virgil wanted to know if Lou Ann had finished her
homework.

12. _____ I can't believe it!

FRIENDLY LETTER

The parts of a friendly letter are the heading, the greeting, the body, the closing, and the signature. The greeting is also called the salutation.

A three-lined formal heading will be used. In informal letters, the date is frequently the only item included. However, the formal heading is important to know.

In a formal letter, as in all formal writing, abbreviations are not used. The **exception** to this is the postal code for states. A postal code is capitalized, and no punctuation is used.

Examples: New Mexico = NM   Maine = ME
Arizona = AZ   Florida = FL

....

FRIENDLY LETTER PARTS:

	POST OFFICE BOX
	or
	HOUSE NUMBER AND STREET NAME
heading	CITY, STATE ZIP CODE
	COMPLETE DATE (not abbreviated)

greeting Dear (Person)   ,

body   The message is written here. Note that you indent at least five letters. You may wish to skip a line between the greeting and the body. Note that you maintain margins on each side of the paper.
   Remember that every time you change topics, you begin a new paragraph.

closing   Your friend,
signature   Writer's Name

....

IMPORTANT NOTES:

1. Notice the **use of commas** in the heading (between city and state), in the greeting, and in the closing. Also, note that **no comma** is placed between the state and the zip code.

2. Capitalize only the first word of a closing. Be sure you know the spelling of *sincerely* and *truly*.

3. Note that the first word of each line of the heading begins at the same place. The same is true of the closing and signature. Also, the heading, closing, and

signature are lined up. You should be able to place a ruler in front of the heading, the closing, and the signature and draw a straight line.

4. Any friendly letter should be spaced down the page. A letter should not be crowded at the top of a page. The number of lines skipped between the heading and body will depend on the length of the message. Again, the letter should be spaced down the page.

5. Be sure to keep margins on both sides of the paper. The heading needs to be set up so that the street name (unabbreviated) will not flow out into the margin.

••

SAMPLE FRIENDLY LETTER:

12321 North Cedar Hill Drive
Scottsdale, AZ 85254
August 14, 20--

Dear Dan and Anne,

We are so excited about your visit this Christmas. Plans are already being made. Our annual Christmas open house is now planned for December 22nd; we want all of our friends to meet you two. Bring some dressy clothes for that occasion. Of course, Christmas Eve service is important to our family. We are glad that you want to attend with us; this is an important night for our family. As we discussed, let's open gifts Christmas morning.

After Christmas, we want to show you our state. If the weather isn't snowy, we'd like to take you to see the Grand Canyon. Prescott and Tucson are interesting. Of course, Phoenix has much to offer, too. I'm sending several brochures so that you can choose what you want to see.

We are so excited about your visit. Let us know what we can do to make this a memorable Christmas vacation.

Love,
Janell

ENVELOPE

The envelope for a friendly letter usually is in block form. That means that each line is exactly below the line before it.

YOUR NAME
HOUSE NUMBER AND STREET ADDRESS **return address**   STAMP

CITY, STATE   ZIP CODE

****

****

PERSON TO WHOM YOU ARE SENDING LETTER
HOUSE NUMBER AND STREET ADDRESS
CITY, STATE   ZIP CODE

Janell Batsworth
5454 East Elm Street
Phoenix, AZ   85032

****
STAMP
****

Mr. and Mrs. Don Landon
4545 East Jackson Way
Clearwater, SC   29822

IMPORTANT NOTES:
1. In a formal envelope, abbreviations are not used.

2. A variation of the block style allows for indentation of each line. If this is chosen, both the return address and the regular address must be indented.

SENTENCES
FRAGMENTS
RUN-ONS

Sentences:

Clauses:
A. **Independent clauses**:
1. An independent clause contains subject and verb.
2. An independent clause expresses a complete thought.
3. An independent clause can stand alone as a sentence.

   Example: Your <u>shirt has</u> some missing buttons.

B. **Dependent clauses**:
1. A dependent clause contains subject and verb.
2. A dependent clause does not express a complete thought.
3. A dependent clause cannot stand alone as a sentence.
4. A dependent clause without an independent clause is a fragment.

   Example: Before <u>you eat</u> lunch.

Fragments:

A. A sentence may be missing a subject. This creates a fragment.

   Example: A running down the street.

B. A sentence may be missing a verb. This creates a fragment.

   Example: The driver of the speed boat.

C. Some fragments are missing both subject and verb.

   Examples: This.
   Recently.
   In the middle of the night.

D. An imperative sentence (command) is not a fragment. Some commands may be only one word, but the subject is (<u>You</u>) meaning "you understood."

   Examples: Stop!   (<u>You</u>) <u>Stop</u>.

   Hold these, please.   (You) <u>Hold</u> these, please.   219

Run-Ons:

A. A run-on may consist of two independent clauses (sentences) run together.

    Example: This <u>car</u> <u>is</u> dirty <u>we</u> <u>will wash</u> it.

B. A run-on may consist of two independent clauses joined by a comma.

    Example: This <u>car</u> <u>is</u> dirty, <u>we</u> <u>will wash</u> it.

    Note: This is often used incorrectly. Even with the comma, the sentence is still a run-on.

C. A run-on may consist of a group of sentences combined with too many conjunctions.

    Example: Mom bought groceries home **and** we had to carry them in **but** she was in a hurry **and** we had to put them away.

D. A run-on may consist of a group of sentences combined with commas.

    Example: Last year our friends went to Denver, then they went to Colorado Springs, next they went to Utah to see some relatives.

🍓🍓🍓

Correcting Run-ons:

1. **Use a period between the independent clauses (sentences).**

    Example: The car is dirty. We will wash it.

2. **Use a semicolon between the independent clauses (sentences).**

    Example: The car is dirty; we will wash it.

    Note: However, the two sentences must be closely related.
          WRONG: The car is dirty; I like pizza.

3. **Use a comma and a conjunction between the independent clauses.**

    Example: This car is dirty, and we will wash it.

4. **Sometimes, the sentence can be changed.**

    Examples: We will wash the dirty car.
220   Because the car is dirty, we will wash it.

Name_____

Date_____

Directions: Cross out any prepositional phrase(s). Underline the subject once and the verb/verb phrase twice. In the space provided, write S̲ for sentence, F̲ for fragment, and R̲-O̲ for run-on.

Example: __F__ ~~With his brother and friend~~.

1. _____ Down the hall.

2. _____ The sheets and pillowcases.

3. _____ My sister and I.

4. _____ A chimpanzee walked along the wall.

5. _____ A policeman searched a shed and went into the house and he checked the back porch and then left in his car.

6. _____ Standing in line.

7. _____ She peeked into the box, she began to laugh.

8. _____ They visited Mt. Rushmore.

9. _____ Stay with me.

10. _____ The movie director began to speak, everyone looked restless and began to look around and smile at each other and not listen.

11. _____ For the first time in two years.

12. _____ He sits in the park daily.

13. _____ The alarm rang at six, he didn't rise until nine o'clock.

14. _____ Although I like you.

15. _____ Go.

Name_____

Date_____

Directions: Cross out any prepositional phrase(s). Underline the subject once and
the verb/verb phrase twice. In the space provided, write S for sentence, F
for fragment, and R-O for run-on.

Example: ___S___ Clouds rolled in from the west.

1. _____ Before the parade.

2. _____ Yes!

3. _____ When you are finished.

4. _____ Stores were crowded with holiday shoppers.

5. _____ Starred in a musical.

6. _____ The boss and his assistant.

7. _____ We need help this table is too heavy.

8. _____ You are right.

9. _____ Our neighbor mows his lawn and pulls weeds, and then he waters it for
an hour, next he admires it.

10. _____ Get up, please.

11. _____ Went to camp last summer.

12. _____ Her flight leaves at midnight.

13. _____ The American flag is passing, we need to stand.

14. _____ To Kentucky for a convention.

15. _____ Tuning into the radio station during a tornado.

222

PRONOUNS

Pronouns take the place of nouns. They agree in number and gender.

Number: **Austin** and **Hal** visited **their** grandparents. (Two requires their.)

Gender: This means using a female pronoun (she, her) when referring to a girl or woman and using a male pronoun (he, him) when referring to a boy or man.

Examples: **Susan** forgot **her** keys.

He hasn't driven **his** car.

Note: If you aren't sure if the noun is a female or male, you may use *his/her*. However, ***his*** has become acceptable in this situation.

Each **child** must bring his/her birth certificate.
or
Each **child** must bring his birth certificate.

Personal Pronouns:

Nominative Pronouns (Subjective Pronouns)	Objective Pronouns	Possessive Pronouns
I	me	my, mine
he	him	his
she	her	her, hers
you	you	your, yours
it	it	it, its
we	us	our, ours
they	them	their, theirs
who	whom	whose
FUNCTION IN A SENTENCE?	**FUNCTION IN A SENTENCE?**	**FUNCTION IN A SENTENCE?**
1. SUBJECT	1. OBJECT OF THE PREPOSITION	SHOW OWNERSHIP
2. PREDICATE NOMINATIVE	2. DIRECT OBJECT	
	3. INDIRECT OBJECT	

PRONOUNS

The nominative or subjective pronouns are **I**, **he**, **she**, **you**, **it**, **we**, and **they**.
Note that **you** and **it** are in both nominative and objective columns of the pronoun chart. They are considered neutral pronouns and do not change from nominative to objective form.

NOMINATIVE PRONOUNS FUNCTION AS EITHER THE SUBJECT OR PREDICATE NOMINATIVE OF A SENTENCE.

A. **Review of Subjects:**

    The subject of a sentence is <u>who</u> or <u>what</u> the sentence is about.

        Examples: A large <u>banner</u> is hanging over the podium.

                    <u>I</u> cannot draw a penguin well.

B. **Review of Predicate Nominatives:**

    The predicate nominative is a word that occurs in the predicate (after the verb) which means the same as the subject.

        Example: His father is the owner of a small hardware store.
                               P.N.
              His <u>father is</u> the owner ~~of a small hardware store~~.

              Proof: <u>The owner is his father.</u>

Predicate pronouns are extremely important. Always invert the sentence to prove a predicate pronoun. This will help you to use correct pronouns.

Examples: The winner was (she, her).
                The winner was **she**.
                Proof: **She** was the winner.   Incorrect: *Her* was the winner.

                John's dad is (he, him) in the white hat.
                John's dad is **he** ~~in the white hat~~.
                Proof: **He** is John's dad.

With predicate nominatives, do not choose by sound. Always invert the sentence for a proof. (If you have heard incorrect usage long enough, it will sound correct.)

When answering the phone, and responding to the question, "Is **Todd** (Sue) there?"
your response should be, "This (person) is <u>**he (she)**</u>."
224   Proof: <u>He (she) is this person.</u>   Incorrect: Him is this person.

Directions: Cross out any prepositional phrase(s). Underline the subject once and
            the verb/verb phrase twice.

        Example: <u>Has</u> <u>one</u> ~~of the ladies~~ <u>wrapped</u> your gift ~~for charity~~?

1. The fire engine raced to the fire.

2. We should have gone on the picnic.

3. A pail of water is beside the campfire.

4. You cannot take this mug with you.

5. Did Sharon send you a "fax" message?

6. I would rather talk to you later.

7. A stewardess must demonstrate airplane safety.

8. Has he given you a bag of chips for lunch?

9. Benjamin and she are going downtown to the public library.

10. His boots and socks are near the front door.

11. You might try the exercise for ten minutes.

12. It is a very humid day.

13. May Katie and I help you in the kitchen?

14. That woman does not leave her children with a babysitter.

15. Either Royce or she had not removed the clothes from the dryer.

Name_____

Date_____

Directions: Cross out any prepositional phrase(s). Underline the subject once and
the verb/verb phrase twice. Label any predicate nominative-P.N. Write
the proof on the line provided.

                                                            P.N.
Example: The <u>judge</u> for the contest <u>was</u> he.

                    Proof: ___He was the judge.___

1. The first person to the finish line was Sarelle.

    Proof: _____

2. The first person to the finish line was she.

    Proof: _____

3. The winner was _____ (your name).

    Proof: _____

4. The winner was I.

    Proof: _____

5. The hostess is the lady in the blue dress.

    Proof: _____

6. The hostess is she in the blue dress.

    Proof: _____

226

Name_____

Date_____

PRONOUNS
Subject or Predicate
Nominative?

Directions: Write <u>S</u> on the line if the boldfaced pronoun is the subject of the
            sentence. Write <u>PN</u> if the boldfaced pronoun is a predicate nominative.

Suggestion: **Cross out any prepositional phrase(s). Underline the
            subject once and the verb/verb phrase twice. Label any
            predicate nominative-<u>P.N.</u> Using this information, write <u>S</u>
            or <u>P N</u> in the space provided.**

                                                                        P.N.
            Example: __PN__   The last <u>person</u> ~~on the elevator~~ <u>was</u> she.

1. _____   **They** walked along the beach in the moonlight.

2. _____   The lady with the most aluminum cans is **Maggie**.

3. _____   The contestant for the quiz show had been **he**.

4. _____   **You** may change your mind.

5. _____   Later, **I** shall seal the letter to Rae Ellen.

6. _____   At the banquet, **we** sat at the head table.

7. _____   Timothy's teacher is **she** in the red suit.

8. _____   After his bath, **he** wears pajamas.

9. _____   Your biggest fans are **we**.

10. _____   Has **he** ever been bitten by a snake?

11. _____   Her father is that **man** with an umbrella.

12. _____   **It** is a pleasure to know you.

PRONOUNS

OBJECTIVE CASE:

The objective pronouns include me, him, her, you, it, us, them, and whom.

Look at your pronoun chart. There are only two pronouns that are in both the nominative and objective columns: you and it. These are called neutral pronouns.

Objective pronouns function as one of the following objects:
    A.   Object of the Preposition
    B.   Direct Object
    C.   Indirect Object

1.   Review of Object of the Preposition:

    The object of the preposition is the noun or pronoun that follows a preposition:

    Examples: The bag is *under the **bed***.

                  This gift is *from **me***.

2.   Review of Direct Objects:

    A direct object receives the action of the verb.

                                D.O.
    Example: Lucy shoved the ***clothes*** into the drawer.

3.   Review of Indirect Objects:

    The indirect object "indirectly" receives a direct object. "To" or "for" can be inserted mentally before an indirect object.

    Examples: The bride rented each bridesmaid a lovely gown.
                       for   **I.O.**
           The bride rented / each **bridesmaid** a lovely gown.

           Their grandmother sent them some money.
                       to **I.O.**
           Their grandmother sent / **them** some money.

Directions: Cross out any prepositional phrase(s).   Label any object of the
                    preposition-O.P.

                                                        O.P.
        Example: The man ~~without an overcoat~~ is cold.

1.   The lamp is below the fan.

2.   Loni made a baby blanket with a satin fringe.

3.   A chair was placed beside the fireplace.

4.   Let's wait for Louis.

5.   We looked in the closet.

6.   Throughout the day we played games.

7.   A post card from him arrived today.

8.   The children are wading in the stream.

9.   An actor sat beside them during the flight.

10.   This discussion is between Lydia and me.

11.   Set this stand near the door.

12.   The story that the teacher read was about dinosaurs.

13.   After a trip, she is always tired.

14.   Would you like to go with Jack and me?

15.   One of the girls left without her purse.   229

Directions: Cross out any prepositional phrase(s). Underline the subject once and
the verb/verb phrase twice. Label any direct object-D.O.

                                        D.O.
          Example: <u>Stevie</u> <u><u>hit</u></u> the ball ~~to the outfield~~.

1. The goat chews grass.

2. His sister bought a dress.

3. Linda has a cute pig.

4. The carpenters finished the house.

5. A dog followed us home.

6. They decorated cookies for the party.

7. Neil hit me with his ruler.

8. A musician sang a slow song.

9. The milkman put the bottles by the front door.

10. Several monkeys ate bananas for a snack.

11. Some boys made a sand castle with a moat.

12. Harvey sent flowers to his mother.

13. Do you play a guitar?

14. Set this on the table, please.

15. At the end of the year, they chose him to give a speech.

Directions: Cross out any prepositional phrase(s). Underline the subject once and the verb/verb phrase twice. Label a direct object-D.O. Label an indirect object-I.O.

Remember: Before an indirect object, you can mentally insert *to* or *for*.

I.O.   D.O.
Example: <u>Justine</u> <u><u>handed</u></u> Tom a slice ~~of watermelon~~.

1. The brother gave the child a kick under the table.

2. Ollie loaned me a book.

3. A storekeeper sends them a wreath at Christmas.

4. A bride handed her bridesmaid some flowers.

5. Gregg tells us his problems.

6. The doctor wrote her a prescription.

7. Give him your ideas.

8. The director promised Marietta a chance at the leading role.

9. Grandma finds Joey little boats at thrift stores.

10. Gina served the guests an iced dessert.

11. A dentist sent him a bill for one hundred dollars.

12. Their friends gave them a going-away party.

13. Lois's grandmother offers her money for good grades.

14. I baked my friend a cake for his birthday.

15. The agent leased him a store in the new shopping center.

Name_____

Date_____

Directions: A pronoun appears in boldfaced print.   Write the letter that tells how the
pronoun functions in the sentence.

1. _____   **She** has gone.
   A.   subject
   B.   predicate nominative

2. _____   He likes **me**!
   A.   object of the preposition
   B.   direct object
   C.   indirect object

3. _____   Harry received a letter from **him**.
   A.   object of the preposition
   B.   direct object
   C.   indirect object

4. _____   The last one to leave the room was **I**.
   A.   subject
   B.   predicate nominative

5. _____   A businessman sent **them** some free samples.
   A.   object of the preposition
   B.   direct object
   C.   indirect object

6. _____   Lauren met **me** by the entrance to the mall.
   A.   object of the preposition.
   B.   direct object
   C.   indirect object

7. _____   The winner was **she**.
   A.   subject
   B.   predicate nominative

8. _____   Patricia helped **him** with his homework.
   A.   object of the preposition
   B.   direct object
   C.   indirect object

232

Directions: A pronoun appears in boldfaced print. Write the letter that tells how
the pronoun functions in the sentence.

1. _____   Clyde's brother sold **them** a set of drums.
A. object of the preposition
B. direct object
C. indirect object

2. _____   Please don't leave without **him**.
A. object of the preposition
B. direct object
C. indirect object

3. _____   The winner should have been **I**.
A. subject
B. predicate nominative

4. _____   A fiddler played **us** a tune.
A. object of the preposition
B. direct object
C. indirect object

5. _____   Barb and **she** live in Wisconsin.
A. subject
B. predicate nominative

6. _____   Has **he** entered college?
A. subject
B. predicate nominative

7. _____   **You** are so kind.
A. subject   D. direct object
B. predicate nominative   E. indirect object
C. object of the preposition

8. _____   Take **it** and run.
A. subject   D. direct object
B. predicate nominative   E. indirect object
C. object of the preposition

Directions: Select the correct pronoun.

1. Come sit beside (I, me).

2. Donna is going with (she, her)

3. (I, Me) love a sunny day.

4. A small, laughing child chased after (he, him).

5. Have (we, us) been given a key?

6. The first one chosen was (I, me).

7. (They, Them) are having a good time.

8. A guide gave (we, us) a tour.

9. (She, Her) must have plans soon.

10. Please take (I, me) with you.

11. The veteran handed (we, us) a small flag.

12. Did he leave (they, them) in the sink?

13. The most adventurous child is (she, her).

14. Give (I, me) your response.

15. The first batter is (he, him).

Name_____

Date_____

Directions: Select the correct pronoun.

1. (I, Me) have agreed to help.

2. Georgia tossed (they, them) a bag of pretzels.

3. A singer showed (he, him) backstage.

4. Bo's teammates are (they, them) in the red uniforms.

5. The ladies' club presented (they, them) scholarships.

6. The long distance runner zipped past (we, us) at great speed.

7. The new model is (he, him) in the brown shirt.

8. During the investigation, (she, her) talked calmly.

9. Has (he, him) been standing on his head again?

10. A travel agent sends (he, him) special tickets.

11. A receptionist asked (I, me) to be seated.

12. My favorite cousin is (her, she).

13. The letter is from (she, her).

14. (We, Us) answered the door immediately.

15. A fan of that team is (he, him) in the team jersey.

Directions: Select the correct pronoun.

Remember: Place your finger or fingers over the first part of the compound.   Then, reread the sentence and choose the proper pronoun.

(In sentences in the present tense, you may have to add s to the verb.)

Example: Kavi and (he, him) want to stay here.
.... (**He**, Him) want**s** to stay here.

1.   The sun umbrella beside Randy and (I, me) has blown over.

2.   Royce and (I, me) want to learn to fly helicopters.

3.   Mom and (she, her) shop with their children.

4.   The two ladies playing bingo were Brandy's aunt and (she, her).

5.   Mr. Clark sent Darius and (he, him) to Nevada.

6.   The matter is between Jansen and (they, them).

7.   Uncle Alonzo will eat dinner with Vicki and (I, me).

8.   Levi's dad sent Stephi and (we, us) tickets to the game.

9.   The mayor handed Mrs. Begay and (she, her) a trophy.

10.   The company director wrote the managers and (they, them) a letter.

11.   Deka and (she, her) like to do crossword puzzles.

12.   The dog followed Tate and (he, him) to the corner.

13.   A handyman and (she, her) repaired the leak.

14.   The delivery person ran past my friend and (I, me).

15.   His favorite aunts are Jamilla and (she, her).

236

PRONOUNS

The possessive pronouns are:

my, mine
his
her, hers
your, yours
its
our, ours
their, theirs
whose

My, his, her, your, its, our, their and whose are placed before nouns and other pronouns and are often called possessive adjectives.

Examples: Do you have **my** *pencil*?   (noun)

His *wallet* is on the floor?   (noun)

Paula gave **her** favorite *one* away.   (pronoun)

A bird spread **its** *wings*.   (noun)

Our *car* isn't in the driveway.   (noun)

Their *leaders* met at the capitol building.   (noun)

Whose *apron* is this?   (noun)

Mine, **hers**, **yours**, **ours**, and **theirs** do not usually come before the noun or pronoun but refer back in the sentence to it.

Examples: That *pen* is **mine**.

Is the *book* on the shelf **yours**?

The plaid *skirt* is **hers**.

Are those *gerbils* **ours**?

His occurs in the same form at any placement.

Examples: **His** *grandmother* lives in Alabama.

The grilled cheese *sandwich* is **his**.

Possessive Pronouns do NOT have an apostrophe (').

A. <u>It's</u> is not a possessive pronoun. <u>It's</u> is a contraction for it is.

    <u>Its</u> is a possessive pronoun.   Example: The cat licked its paws.

Suggestion: If you are unsure <u>its</u> or <u>it's</u> should be used in a sentence, read the sentence with the *it is* form. Trust sound to determine your choice.

    Examples: It's hot.
              Check: It is hot.

           The cat licked it's paws.
                Check: The cat licked it is paws.
              Correct: The cat licked its paws.

B. <u>You're</u> is not a possessive pronoun. <u>You're</u> is a contraction for *you are*.

<u>Your</u> is a possessive pronoun.   Example: Where is your coat?

Suggestion: If you are unsure <u>you're</u> or <u>your</u> should be used, read the sentence with the *you are* form.   Trust sound to determine your choice.

    Examples: You're so funny.
               Check: You are so funny.

           Is that you're candy?
                Check: Is that you are candy?
              Correct: Is that your candy?

C. <u>They're</u> is not a possessive pronoun. <u>They're</u> is a contraction for they are.

<u>Their</u> is a possessive pronoun.   Example: Their coach talked to them.

Suggestion: If you are unsure <u>they're</u> or <u>their</u> should be used, read the sentence with the *they are* form. Trust sound to determine your choice.

    Examples: They're leaving now.
             Check: They are leaving now.

           They're dad is a plumber.
                Check: They are dad is a plumber.
              Correct: Their dad is a plumber.

Name_____

Date_____

Directions: Select the correct word.

Suggestion: Say each sentence separating the contraction.
Use this method to determine your choice.

Example: Do you want to know if (its, it's) ear is infected?

Do you want to know if it is ear is infected?   Wrong!

The answer is **its**.

1.   (It's, Its) a great day.

2.   I hope (their, they're) coming soon.

3.   (You're, Your) elbow has black smudges on it.

4.   Have you seen (their, they're) first home?

5.   (You're, Your) welcome to stay.

6.   A monkey scratched under (its, it's) arm.

7.   (Their, They're) toilet overflowed.

8.   Ask if (their, they're) ready.

9.   I would like (your, you're) opinion on this.

10.   The dog stopped wagging (its, it's) tail.

11.   (You're, Your) the best skater he has seen.

12.   He has (their, they're) photographs from camp.

Name_____   **PRONOUNS**

Date_____

Directions: Select the correct word.

Suggestion: Say each sentence separating the contraction.
Use this method to determine your choice.

Example: Kenneth and Andrea like (their, they're) new home.

Kenneth and Andrea like they are new home.   Wrong!

The answer is **their**.

1.   During the high wind, (their, they're) chairs blew over.

2.   (It's, Its) nice to meet you.

3.   Do you know that (your, you're) the winner?

4.   Has anyone taken (your, you're) temperature?

5.   (Their, They're) finished!

6.   (It's, Its) wings are damaged.

7.   A hamster snuggled in the corner of (its, it's) cage.

8.   (Your, You're) kidding me!

9.   Sally is (their, they're) friend.

10.   His mother and (your, you're) sister are working at the same place.

11.   I believe that (they're, their) helping with the move.

12.   Do you wonder how (its, it's) possible?

PRONOUNS

Reflexive Pronouns:

Reflexive pronouns end with **self** or **selves**. Reflexive pronouns are **myself**, **himself**, **herself**, **itself**, **yourself**, **ourselves**, and **themselves**.

Hisself and theirselves are incorrect. DO NOT USE THEM!

Reflexive pronouns reflect back to another noun or pronoun in a sentence. (The word to which a reflexive pronoun refers back is called an <u>antecedent</u>.)

Examples: I will do it **myself**.

Ginny finished the job **herself**.

His dad did the roofing **himself**.

Help **yourself** to the food.

The cat licked **itself**.

We want to try it **ourselves**.

They bought all the food for the trip **themselves**.

Antecedents:

An antecedent is the noun or pronoun to which a possessive or a reflexive pronoun refers in a sentence.

Possessives:

    A. The man built a large chest for <u>his</u> son.

        1. <u>His</u> refers back to **man**. (The man built a large chest for the man's son.)
        2. **Man** is the noun to which <u>his</u> refers back in the sentence.
        3. **Man** is the antecedent.

    B. The boys splashed their friends with a hose.

        1. <u>Their</u> refers back to boys. (The boys splashed the boys' friends with a hose.)
        2. **Boys** is the noun to which <u>their</u> refers back in the sentence.
        3. **Boys** is the antecedent.

Reflexives:

    A. The kite wrapped <u>itself</u> around a pole.

        1. <u>Itself</u> is the reflexive pronoun.
        2. <u>Itself</u> refers back to **kite**.
        3. **Kite** is the antecedent.

    B. We need to clean ourselves.

        1. <u>Ourselves</u> is the reflexive pronoun.
        2. <u>Ourselves</u> refers back to **we**.
        3. **We** (a pronoun) is the antecedent.

Note: An antecedent will not be a word in a prepositional phrase.
        The bird with the broken wing hurt its leg as well.
        The bird ~~with the broken wing~~ hurt **its** leg as well.
                antecedent for its = bird

Directions: Select the reflexive pronoun in each sentence.

1. Let Jolynn find it herself.

2. I need to go myself.

3. Lionel washes his dog himself.

4. The guests enjoyed themselves.

5. Mickey and I want to listen to the recording ourselves.

6. Nita wants to do it herself.

7. A little robin perched itself on a branch.

8. The lady muttered to herself about the weather.

9. The boys hauled the stones themselves.

10. We, ourselves, must make the decision.

11. May I do it myself?

12. One of the boys made himself a huge sandwich.

13. A dog chased itself in the mirror.

14. Phillip and we managed to do that ourselves.

15. Many people volunteer themselves for feeding the hungry.

Date_____

Directions: Write the antecedent for the underlined word on the line.

Example: _____Bridgette_____   Bridgette left <u>her</u> books in the truck.

1. _____   Dad put <u>his</u> tool down.

2. _____   I don't know where <u>my</u> sweater is.

3. _____   The girls gave <u>their</u> mom a hug.

4. _____   A small lizard stuck <u>its</u> tongue out.

5. _____   Janie does house painting <u>herself</u>.

6. _____   Yul and I don't want <u>our</u> picture taken.

7. _____   You must fix this <u>yourself</u>.

8. _____   Some dogs were lying by <u>their</u> bowls.

9. _____   Several men built a church <u>themselves</u>.

10. _____   Adam must bake a birthday cake <u>himself</u>.

11. _____   He found <u>his</u> water gun in the bottom drawer.

12. _____   I will find the way <u>myself</u>.

Date_____

Directions: Write the antecedent for the underlined word on the line.

Example: _____He_____ He wants to dig the hole <u>himself</u>.

1. _____ Hal and she drove all the way <u>themselves</u>.

2. _____ A bird fluttered <u>its</u> wings and flew off.

3. _____ The teenager wants to buy a car <u>himself</u>.

4. _____ Misha and I left <u>our</u> umbrellas on the bus.

5. _____ A waiter gave us <u>his</u> pen.

6. _____ Lea needs to give <u>her</u> pet rabbit some food.

7. _____ Marta and she are giving <u>their</u> time to help.

8. _____ History often repeats <u>itself</u>.

9. _____ I am throwing <u>my</u> old notebook away.

10. _____ Amanda gave Nam <u>her</u> notes.

11. _____ The model washes <u>herself</u> with a special soap.

12. _____ Cyrus and he dished out <u>their</u> lunches.

PRONOUNS

Demonstrative Pronouns:

The demonstrative pronouns are **this**, **that**, **those**, and **these**.

      Examples: **This** was a terrific idea!

               Will you please give **that** away?

               Are you sure **those** are the ones you want?

               These are a great buy!

≈≈≈

Note: Them is not a demonstrative pronoun.

    Incorrect: Them surely are pretty.   Incorrect: I like them shoes.

      Correct: Those surely are pretty.   Correct: I like those shoes.

≈≈≈

If **this**, **that**, **those**, and **these** modify (go over to) a noun or pronoun, they function as adjectives.

      Examples: **This** is terrible.   (pronoun)

               This spaghetti is terrible. (adjective: this spaghetti)

               He bought **that** at a sale. (pronoun)

               He bought **that** tire at a sale.   (adjective: that tire)

               Are **those** yours? (pronouns)

               Are **those** socks yours? (adjective: those socks)

               I like **these**. (pronoun)

246   I like **these** chewy bars. (adjective: these bars)

Name_____

Date_____

Directions: Write <u>P</u> on the line if the underlined word serves as a pronoun; write <u>A</u> if the underlined word serves as an adjective. Write the adjective and the noun it modifies on the line after the sentence. A sentence marked <u>P</u> will be blank.

Example: __P__   Try <u>these</u>!   _____

1. _____   <u>This</u> rug is a Native American one.   _____

2. _____   Please hand me <u>that</u>.   _____

3. _____   <u>Those</u> machines are complicated.   _____

4. _____   We laugh often about <u>that</u>.   _____

5. _____   Are <u>these</u> what you had in mind?   _____

6. _____   You may want to read <u>this</u> article.   _____

7. _____   Would you like <u>that</u> heated?   _____

8. _____   Henry collected <u>these</u> shells on vacation._____

9. _____   You may remove <u>that</u> label from the shirt._____

10. _____   <u>This</u> stereo has superb sound.   _____

11. _____   I can't seem to do anything with <u>this</u>.   _____

12. _____   Are <u>these</u> coins rare?   _____

13. _____   <u>That</u> curling iron is very hot.   _____

14. _____   We would like two of <u>those</u>.   _____

15. _____   Zachary removed <u>these</u> with worn pages from the library shelves.

_____

PRONOUNS

Interrogative Pronouns:

Interrogative pronouns ask a question.
Interrogative pronouns are **who**, **whom**, **whose**, **which**, and **what**.

        Examples: **Who** is that?

                     To **whom** did you give the money?

                     Whose is this?

                     Which do you want?

                     What is your name?

Who is in the nominative case and will function as the subject or predicate nominative of a sentence.

        Who is your best friend?   (subject)

        The new minister is **who**?   (predicate nominative)
        Proof: <u>Who is the new minister?</u>

Whom is in the objective case and will function as the direct object, indirect object, and object of the preposition. (**Use <u>whom</u> after *to, for,* and *with.*)**

        For **whom** did you make this?   (object of the preposition)

        You called **whom**?   (direct object)

        Miss Lilt sent **whom** a post card?   (indirect object)

<u>Whose</u>, <u>which</u>, and <u>what</u> are pronouns when they stand alone. However, if they modify (go over to) a noun or another pronoun, they function as adjectives.

        Examples: **Whose** is this?   (pronoun)
                    Whose book is this?   (adjective)

                    Which do you want?   (pronoun)
                    Which one do you want? (adjective)

                    What should I do?   (pronoun)
248   **What** activity should I do? (adjective)

Directions: Write <u>P</u> on the line if the boldfaced word serves as a pronoun; write <u>A</u> on the line if the boldfaced word serves as an adjective.

Example: __A__   **Which** shirt did you buy?

1.   _____   **Which** snake is poisonous?

2.   _____   **Whose** is this?

3.   _____   **What** have I done?

4.   _____   **What** phone number did you dial?

5.   _____   **Whose** cookies are these?

6.   _____   **Which** van do you like?

7.   _____   **What** answer did he give?

8.   _____   **Which** do you want?

9.   _____   **Whose** are these?

10.   _____   **What** animal do you like best?

Directions: Select the correct answer.

Note: Use *whom* after <u>to,</u> <u>for,</u> or <u>with</u>:

1.   (Who, Whom) was with you?

2.   To (who, whom) did you speak?

3.   (Who, Whom) is your favorite?

4.   From (who, whom) did you receive the gift?

5.   The last person in line was (who, whom)?

PRONOUNS

Indefinite Pronouns:

Indefinite pronouns are **some**, **many**, **few**, **several**, **each**, **both**, **either**, **neither**, **someone**, **somebody**, **anyone**, **nobody**, **everyone**, **everybody**, **any**, and **none**.

Examples: **Some** are in the laundry.

                  Many will be attending the party.

                  A **few** won't be going.

                  Each must bring his own lunch.

                  I want **both**.

                  You may choose **either**.

                  Neither is going.

                  Please share this with **someone.**

                  Somebody left this.

                  Has **anyone** seen Kathleen?

                  They don't want **anybody** to know.

                  Nobody wants to go.

                  Everyone is here.

                  He likes **everybody**.

                  Do you have **any**?

                  I want **none**, thanks.

Pronoun or Adjective:

If **some**, **many**, **few**, **several**, **each**, **both**, **either**, **neither**, **someone's**, **somebody's**, **anyone's**, **anybody's**, **nobody's**, **everyone's**, **everybody's**, or **any** modify (go over to) a noun or pronoun, that word functions as an adjective.

Examples: **Several** bunnies hopped into a hole.

                  She doesn't want to hear **anyone's** story.

250   I don't like **either** wallpaper.

Name_____

Date_____

Directions: Place P on the line if the underlined word serves as a pronoun; write A on the line if the underlined word serves as an adjective. Write the adjective and the noun it modifies on the line after the sentence.   A sentence marked P will be blank.

Example: ___A___   A <u>few</u> lions prowled around while others slept. <u>few lions</u>

1. _____   <u>Some</u> people enjoy Japanese food.   _____

2. _____   Please give me <u>some</u>.   _____

3. _____   <u>Each</u> must choose a bed.   _____

4. _____   <u>Each</u> partner may take his turn.   _____

5. _____   Are there <u>many</u> straws in that package?_____

6. _____   Have <u>many</u> visited Arlington Cemetery?_____

7. _____   <u>Both</u> want to be teachers.   _____

8. _____   <u>Both</u> men decided to play tennis.   _____

9. _____   I've tried <u>several</u> different mustards.   _____

10. _____   Are there <u>several</u> in the bin?   _____

11. _____   Has <u>anyone</u> done the dishes?   _____

12. _____   Did <u>anyone's</u> parents come to the meeting? _____

13. _____   <u>Either</u> boy may come with me.   _____

14. _____   I don't want <u>either</u>.   _____

15. _____   Do you have <u>any</u> pets?   _____

PRONOUNS

A. Often <u>we</u> or <u>us</u> will appear beside a noun. In order to determine which to use, place your finger over the noun following it. Then, decide according to how the word functions in the sentence.

    1. (We, Us) girls like to talk together.
       (**We**, Us)   like to talk together.   (subject)

    2. Give (we, us) adults a chance to play, too.
       Give (we, **us**)   a chance to play, too.   (indirect object)

    3. The lucky ones were (we, us) boys.
       The lucky ones were (**we**, us).   (predicate nominative)
       Proof: <u>We were the lucky ones</u>.

B. If an indefinite pronoun is plural, the possessive following it needs to be plural.

    Many sent **their** best wishes.   (<u>Many</u> is called the antecedent.)

    Both want **their** baseballs autographed.   (<u>Both</u> is called the antecedent.)

If an indefinite pronoun is singular, the possessive following it needs to be singular.

    Each wants **his** turn at the bumper cars.   (<u>Each</u> is called the antecedent.)

    Everyone is taking **her** bathing suit.   (<u>Everyone</u> is called the antecedent.)

    Note: Everyone may sound plural; however, it is singular.
           If it were plural, we would say, "Everyone are going." Of course, we say, "Everyone is going."

           Everyone is taking **her**, *not their*, bathing suit.

C. Cross out prepositional phrase(s). This will help you to determine which possessive is needed.

    Each ~~of the children~~ is waiting **his** turn.   (<u>Each</u> is called the antecedent.)

    This may "sound" wrong; however **his** is singular because the pronoun **each** is singular.

252

Name_____

Date_____

A. Directions: Select the correct pronoun.

1. Do you want (we, us) teammates to keep score?

2. (We, Us) friends will plan to stay together.

3. The elephant came near (we, us) children at the zoo.

4. The coach gave (we, us) winners trophies.

5. The best people to do that job are (we, us) girls.

6. (We, Us) workers need a raise.

7. Leave (we, us) players alone.

8. Would you like to come with (we, us) teenagers?

B. Directions: Select the correct pronoun.

1. Several set (his, their) bags on the ground.

2. Everyone must take (his, their) books.

3. Many decided to keep (his, their) own money.

4. Each of the girls must take (her, their) hat.

5. Nobody wants (his, their) picture taken.

6. Both have chosen (his, their) vehicles carefully.

7. Everyone of the men took (his, their) time.

8. Somebody needs to look at (his, their) watch.

Name_____   **PRONOUN REVIEW**

Date_____

A. Directions: Write <u>S</u> if the pronoun in boldfaced print functions as the subject; write
                  <u>PN</u> if the pronoun in boldfaced print functions as a predicate
                  nominative.

Suggestion: **Cross out any prepositional phrase(s). Underline the subject once and the
              verb/verb phrase twice.   Then, make your decision.**

Remember: Invert the sentence to prove a predicate nominative.

1. _____   **We** are sleeping in a tent.

2. _____   In the afternoon, **he** walks two miles.

3. _____   The person receiving the award is **she**.

4. _____   Our neighbors are **they** by the flag pole.

5. _____   Soon, **I** shall find it.

B. Directions: Choose the letter that tells how the pronoun functions in the sentence.

1. _____   The newscaster wants to go with **him**.
               a.   object of the preposition
               b.   direct object
               c.   indirect object

2. _____   You hit **me**!
               a.   object of the preposition
               b.   direct object
               c.   indirect object

3. _____   **She** sings constantly.
               a.   subject
               b.   predicate nominative

4. _____   The banker will give **them** the loan for a car.
               a.   object of the preposition
               b.   direct object
               c.   indirect object

254

C.   Directions: Select the correct pronoun.

1.   (They, Them) need a ride.

2.   (Him, He) likes to sleep late.

3.   I can't find (she, her).

4.   Take (they, them) with you.

5.   The red team will play against (us, we) later.

6.   The best choice is (him, he).

7.   That book belongs to (me, I).

D.   Directions: Select the correct pronoun.

Suggestion: You may want to place your finger over the first part of the compound.

1.   Johnny and (I, me) left late.

2.   A dog wandered over and sat beside Mack and (he, him).

3.   A large glass of iced tea had been served to her friend and (she, her).

4.   The graduating seniors from that area are Cody and (he, him).

5.   Spectators watched the leader and (them, they) water ski.

6.   He didn't give that team or (we, us) a chance.

E.   Directions: Select the correct word.

1.   (Their, They're) having fun.

2.   I wonder why the gerbil runs around in (it's, its) cage.

3.   Is (their, they're) dad a computer expert?

4.   We hope that (your, you're) chosen.

Name_____   **PRONOUN REVIEW**

Date_____

F.   Directions: Fill in the blank.

1.   Write an example of a reflexive pronoun. _____

2.   An example of a demonstrative pronoun is _____, and an example of an interrogative pronoun is _____.

3.   Write two indefinite pronouns. _____ and _____

G.   Directions: Write the antecedent of the underlined pronoun.

1. _____   Mom irons <u>her</u> tablecloths.

2. _____   I can't do this <u>myself</u>.

3. _____   Lani and Al want <u>their</u> marbles back.

4. _____   One girl carried <u>her</u> own moving boxes.

5. _____   We don't have <u>our</u> pets along.

H.   Directions: Write <u>A</u> if the underlined word functions as an adjective; write <u>P</u> if the underlined word functions as a pronoun.

1. _____   Mrs. Hanson wants <u>those</u>.

2. _____   Are <u>those</u> cups dirty?

3. _____   <u>Which</u> pear is yours?

4. _____   <u>Which</u> does he want?

5. _____   Are there <u>many</u> left?

6. _____   <u>Many</u> balloons had been blown up for the party.

7. _____   <u>That</u> is unbelievable!

8. _____   Are you sure <u>that</u> story is true?

9. _____   We'd like <u>some</u> water, please.

256   10. _____   Would you like <u>some</u>?

Name_____

Date_____

I. Directions: Select the correct pronoun.

1. My aunt is (she, her) with my dad.

2. A boy sat by (himself, hisself).

3. Give (they, them) a minute to locate it.

4. Have Harold and (him, he) walked home?

5. A ringmaster lifted (his, their) megaphone.

6. With (who, whom) has Janice gone?

7. Teddy gave Breck and (she, her) some rubber bands.

8. Mrs. Thompson and (me, I) will sign those papers.

9. (We, Us) boys played games all afternoon.

10. Truman and (us, we) are writing songs.

11. (Who, Whom) is the author of <u>Summer of the Monkeys</u>?

12. One of the blue jays lost a few of (their, its) feathers.

13. Please loan (we, us) actors your old chest for a prop.

14. To (who, whom) should this be sent?

15. Your friend is (who, whom)?

16. Split the candy between Gary and (I, me).

Name_____   **CUMULATIVE REVIEW**

Date_____

A. Directions: Cross out any prepositional phrase(s). Underline the subject once
    and the verb/verb phrase twice. Label any direct object-<u>D.O.</u>; label
    any indirect object-<u>I.O.</u>

1. The father with the twins looks happy.

2. At the beginning of the year, Earl changed jobs.

3. The zoo keeper and his helper feed the animals.

4. An owner of a restaurant offered his customers free sodas.

5. One of the women stood and clapped her hands.

6. Put this coin into your pocket.

B. Directions: Cross out any prepositional phrase(s). Underline the subject once
    and the verb/verb phrase twice. Label any direct object-<u>D.O.</u>

1. Have you (took, taken) your brother to that performance?

2. He should have (swam, swum) another lap.

3. Her mother-in-law could not have (came, come) earlier.

4. I must have (drank, drunk) too much water.

5. The mother and son had (gone, went) to a puppet show.

6. You might have (brung, brought) something to eat.

7. The cat has (laid, lain) on the bed for an hour.

8. Some ladies (rose, raised) their hands to vote.

9. Please (sit, set) here beside me.

10. (May, Can) we eat popsicles now?
258

Date_____

C. Directions: Write <u>A</u> if the verb is action; write <u>L</u> if the verb is linking.

Suggestion: **Write *is, am, are, was,* or *were* above a verb that is on the linking list. If the meaning of the sentence is not changed, the verb is probably linking.**

1. _____   After the fire, the fireman looked exhausted.

2. _____   She looked his way and smiled.

3. _____   The bell sounded and then stopped suddenly.

4. _____   This gourd sounds hollow.

D. Directions: Write the contraction.

1. how is - _____   5. they have - _____

2. we were - _____   6. do not - _____

3. had not - _____   7. I am - _____

4. cannot - _____   8. will not - _____

E. Directions: Cross out any prepositional phrase(s). Underline the subject once and the verb/verb phrase twice. On the line, write the tense, *present, past,* or *future,* in the space provided.

1. _____   A crossing guard helps the children.

2. _____   The children will build houses with sugar cubes.

3. _____   Toby dusted his room.

4. _____   They make gingerbread houses each Christmas.

F. Directions: Write intj. above each interjection.

1. Wow! It's all gone!

2. They're here! Yeah!

G.   Directions: Label any conjunction.

1.   Timothy or Gary developed the plan.

2.   My brother and I are coming, but we can't stay long.

H.   Directions: Write <u>A</u> if the noun is abstract; write <u>C</u> if the noun is concrete.

1. _____   mole   2. _____   joy   3. _____   file   4. _____   wisdom

I.   Directions: Write <u>C</u> if the noun is common; write <u>P</u> if the noun is proper.

1. _____   STREET   3. _____   WOMAN   5. _____   AMY GRANT

2. _____   ASH STREET   4. _____   SINGER   6. _____   MT. SHASTA

J.   Directions: Write <u>N</u> if the underlined word functions as a noun; write <u>A</u> if the underlined word functions as an adjective.

1. _____   A <u>post</u> had been decorated with crepe paper.

2. _____   Please send me a <u>post</u> card.

3. _____   That man wears a <u>bow</u> tie.

4. _____   Her hair <u>bow</u> is purple.

K.   Directions: Write <u>N</u> if the underlined word functions as a noun; write <u>V</u> if the underlined word functions as a verb.

1. _____   Will you <u>nail</u> these boards together?

2. _____   One <u>nail</u> is needed to finish the jewelry box.

3. _____   A <u>roll</u> with jelly was served.

4. _____   They <u>roll</u> dough for sugar cookies.

Name_____   **CUMULATIVE REVIEW**

Date_____

L.   Directions: Write the possessive form.

1.   a shopping cart belonging to a store - _____

2.   dolls belonging to three girls - _____

3.   a luncheon shared by more than one woman - _____

4.   a path used by horses - _____

M.   Directions: Write the plural of each noun.

1. dish - _____   3. lime - _____   5. match - _____

2. mouse - _____   4. leaf - _____   6. goose - _____

N.   Directions: Box nouns.

1.   A container of yogurt is in the refrigerator.

2.   Several diners ate two pieces of cherry pie.

3.   I would like glazed carrots, several pickled eggs, and a slice of Carole's cake.

4.   Their sister placed an arrangement of tulips on that table.

5.   This cap and your old hat need to be washed in this gadget.

O.   Directions: Underline the subject once and the verb/verb phrase twice.   Label
                any predicate nominative-<u>P.N.</u>   Write the proof on the line.

1.   Miss Lewis is a teacher at Baltic School.

     Proof: _____

2.   <u>Where the Red Fern Grows</u> is a famous book.

     Proof: _____

3.   Travis is the boy with the snake.

     Proof: _____

Name_____   **CUMULATIVE REVIEW**

Date_____

P. Directions: Circle any adjective(s).
Remember: Read the sentence and circle limiting adjectives first.   Then, circle descriptive adjectives.

1. Was the first California mission at San Diego?

2. One person ordered two pork chops and fried okra for dinner.

3. Her older sister is an usher for a welcome club.

4. Their principal visited a Japanese school last year.

5. Marv's new beige slacks have black ink on the right cuff.

Q. Directions: Select the correct adjective form.

1. He is (taller, tallest) than I.

2. Ray is the (louder, loudest) singer in the trio.

3. Brian is (more talkative, most talkative) than his partner.

4. Mr. Lyons is the (more successful, most successful) lawyer in his office.

5. I was (more courageous, most courageous) on my second try.

R. Directions: Read each group of words. Write S for sentence, F for fragment, and R-O for run-on.
Suggestion: Cross out any prepositional phrases, underline the subject once and the verb/verb phrase twice. This helps greatly in making a choice.

1. _____   A ground hog came out of its hole and ran across the meadow, then headed toward a woods, but turned around and it scampered back into its hole.

2. _____   A waffle iron in the kitchen.

3. _____   Sid sometimes reads during his break at work.

4. _____   Nelson continued to run, we ran after him.

262

S. Directions: Write the sentence type: declarative (statement), interrogative (question), imperative (command), and exclamatory.

1. _____ Please hurry.

2. _____ The dog needs to be fed.

3. _____ Has the nurse taken his blood pressure?

4. _____ Wow! You received it!

T. Directions: Select the correct adverb.

1. You should chew your food (good, well),

2. The limousine driver opened the door (slow, slowly).

3. His science project took (longer, longest) than yours.

4. This washing machine buzzes (more shrilly, most shrilly) than the old one.

5. Don't act so (weird, weirdly).

U. Directions: Circle any adverb(s).

Suggestion: Cross out any prepositional phrase(s). Underline the subject once and the verb/verb phrase twice. Look for any adverb that tells <u>to what extent</u>. Then, go back and look for any adverb(s) that tell <u>how</u>. Next, look for any adverb(s) that tell <u>when</u>. Then, search for any adverb(s) that tell <u>where</u>.

1. When will you arrive there?

2. His injured finger hurt quite badly.

3. Tomorrow, the library will open early.

4. Lester cannot find his bag anywhere in his room.

5. They are always home on Saturday.

6. He took the dessert out of the refrigerator too soon.

CAPITALIZATION

RULE 1: **Capitalize the first letter of the first word in a sentence.**

Example: Chicken was baked in an oven.

RULE 2: **Capitalize the pronoun I.**

Example: Should I call you later?

RULE 3: **Capitalize the first letter of the first word in most lines of poetry.**

Example: She always thought a gallant prince would love her,
Forsaking life itself to please only her.

RULE 4: **Capitalize the first word, the last word, and all important words in any title. Do not capitalize a, an, the, and, but, or, nor, or prepositions of four or less letters unless they are the first or last word of a title.** (*Memorize this entire rule!*)

Examples: "Silence of the Songbirds"

"Missiles to Earth from a Crater on Mars"

Be sure to capitalize all verbs in titles.

Example: "You *Are* My Sunshine"

Be sure to capitalize prepositions of five or more letters in titles.

Example: The Man *Without* a Country

RULE 5: **Capitalize people's names and their initial(s).**

Examples: Sharon

Directions: Write the capital letter above any word that needs to be capitalized.

                                 H   T
                Example: has tommy finished?

1. are chanda and i invited?

2. the musical, <u>oklahoma</u>, has been performed many times.

3. do i need to sing "amazing grace" with you?

4. lani and i will read this magazine, <u>puppy playtime</u>.

5. his mother read him <u>goldilocks and the three bears</u>.

6. the movie, <u>lassie, come home</u>, is an old one.

7. (poem)   "eagle"

                perched upon a ledge,
                gold eyes,
                searching wisely

8. mr. jones reads the <u>bible</u> daily.

9. her favorite poem is "if" by rudyard kipling.

10. we read the book entitled <u>new mexico is for kids</u> by bobbi salts.

11. a grandmother sang "everything is beautiful" to the child.

12. dad enjoyed reading <u>hope for the troubled heart</u> by billy graham.

13. miss ving entitled her speech "living within your budget".

14. deven, elijah, and caleb wrote a song entitled "we are funny".

15. the poem "why nobody pets the lion at the zoo" is by john ciardi.

Name_____ **CAPITALIZATION**

Date_____

Directions: Write the capital letter above any word that needs to be capitalized.

Example: last summer i read <u>the greatest miracle in the world</u>.
(capital letters shown above: L   I   T G   M   W)

1.   the only two people who came were breck and i.

2.   robert frost wrote "at woodwards's garden."

3.   did carl sandburg write the poem entitled "see the trees"?

4.   "travel"

                        by robert louis stevenson

                  i should like to rise and go
                  where the golden apples grow.

5.   billy coleman is the main character of <u>where the red fern grows</u>.

6.   roger and i like children's books with colored pictures.

7.   "an old woman of the road" is a poem with six stanzas.

8.   have you read "the lady or the tiger" by stockton?

9.   did miss logan, regan, or i upset you?

10.   the class was assigned "the truth about thunderstorms."

11.   who wrote, "when icicles hang on the wall"?

12.   may i read your <u>phoenix gazette</u> newspaper?

13.   she and her cousin watched the movie, <u>fiddler on the roof</u>.

14.   my mother read <u>survival for busy women</u> by emilie barnes.

15.   the title of michelle's essay was "a glance through jefferson's eyes."

RULE 6: **Capitalize days, months, holidays, and special days.**

      Examples: Tuesday   Thanksgiving

                      July   Arbor Day

                      Hanukkah   St. Patrick's Day

                      Christmas Eve   Sunday

RULE 7: **Capitalize Mother, Dad, and other titles if you can insert the person's name.**

      Examples: Has Dad gone to the store?

                      (If Mike is the father's name: Has Mike gone to the store?)
                      You can replace Dad with a name; therefore, you capitalize
                      Dad.

                      My mom is nice.
                      (If Amy is the mother's name: My Amy is nice.)
                      This doesn't make sense; therefore, you do not capitalize
                      mom.

Capitalize the title if it appears with a name.

        Examples: Uncle Duane

                        Aunt Fran

                        Grandma Wilson

                        Lieutenant Jackson

RULE 8: **Capitalize names of organizations.**

      Examples: Future Homemakers of America

                      American Red Cross

                      Organization of American States

Directions: Write the capital letter above any word that needs to be capitalized.

                I M
     Example: is monday the last day of the trip?

1.   please ask dad to help us.

2.   does grandpa grovers belong to the lion's club?

3.   is uncle alvin a leader of the boy scouts of america?

4.   next friday we will celebrate columbus day.

5.   my mother has joined the tulsa women's club.

6.   was aunt jean born on st. valentine's day?

7.   yesterday, judge lipman announced the verdict.

8.   every wednesday, grandma and professor stone have lunch.

9.   is independence day celebrated on july 4th?

10.   in march, general frampton will speak to their class.

11.   her mother belongs to concerned women of america*.

12.   has mayor lexico talked with members of the chandler chamber of commerce*?

13.   we learned that uncle don and aunt joy will come for a visit at christmas.

14.   garth, nancy, and cousin linda discussed pollution with senator parks.

15.   during the st. patrick's day celebration, my grandfather wore green.

*name of an organization

Date_____

Directions: Write the capital letter above any word that needs to be capitalized.

                          W   J
Example: will your grandfather go with us in june?

1. at the christmas eve service, pastor gilman gave a sermon.

2. no one wanted captain adams or dad to leave.

3. have you seen my mother or principal grady here?

4. his father joined an organization called parents without partners.

5. the carnival was held the last saturday of august.

6. aaron and i are planning a party for april fool's day.

7. was president george washington sworn into office in january?

8. aunt lisa and her sister will be here on the weekend after labor day.

9. is veteran's day always celebrated on november 11th?

10. representative irving will be on a television show on thursday.

11. the national rifle association made a comment about hand guns.

12. we gave mom a rose for her mothers' day present.

13. has your grandmother ever visited during the thanksgiving holiday?

14. how long has doctor joan carney belonged to the american medical association?

15. tell your cousin to meet us sunday at our church to celebrate palm sunday.

RULE 9: **Capitalize the names of institutions.**

Morton School   Samaritan Hospital

York College   Maricopa County Jail

RULE 10: **Capitalize business names.**

Cross Company   Sock Store, Inc.

Ameriola Airlines   Murray Hotel

Beamer Grocery   Posada Restaurant

RULE 11: **Capitalize the names of structures.**

Washington Tunnel   Leaning Tower of Pisa

London Bridge   Cumberland Expressway

RULE 12: **Capitalize the names of specific geographic places.**

Indian Ocean   North America

Baltic Sea   England

Missouri River   Maryland

Skunk Creek   Fulton County

Pocono Mountains   Memphis

Mt. Rushmore   Mammoth Cave

Fox Hill   Dristol Park

Roanoke Island   Cape Cod

Gulf of Mexico   Midwest

Date_____

Directions: Write the capital letter above any word that needs to be capitalized.

                 W   D   P
    Example: we like to go to dorado park.

1.   is the george washington bridge in new york?

2.   he is in memorial hospital on market street.

3.   the grand canyon is in arizona.

4.   the leader of arki industries is mr. james horton.

5.   a group went to washington and fished in the columbia river.

6.   is victoria falls on the continent of africa?

7.   they flew over the arctic circle on their way to germany.

8.   has lionel ever attended franklin school on milton avenue?

9.   the class toured desert horizon police station in phoenix.

10.   a post card from florence prison arrived on tuesday.

11.   when miss harlord was in asia, she visited the great wall of china.

12.   is mustang library on bristol road or shea boulevard?

13.   the flight for america north airlines was early.

14.   the family crossed the rio grande river and drove into mexico.

15.   a girl from the south plans on going to hoover dam in nevada.

Directions: Write the capital letter above any word that needs to be capitalized.

                  T E   C   F   E
     Example: the english channel separates france and england.

1. have you been to moosehead lake in maine?

2. the butte mountains and black rock desert are in nevada.

3. portia blanderson calls her company cottage cleaning, inc.

4. joan attended a junior high school before entering sunburst middle school.

5. the world trade center in new york city is very famous.

6. the town of barnsdall is in osage county, oklahoma.

7. the new location of coe restaurant is on walker avenue.

8. is great smoky mountains national park in north carolina?

9. a place called bowers beach is on the delaware bay in delaware.

10. last year their family went to wrigley field in chicago for a baseball game.

11. has anyone visited the kennedy center in washington, d. c.?

12. art traveled to the town of fish haven on bear lake, idaho.

13. did you know that homosassa island is in the gulf of mexico?

14. the tappan zee bridge in new york crosses the hudson river.

15. do students from gettysburg college sometimes lunch at wolfe's diner?

RULE 13: **Capitalize the names of historical events and historical documents (papers).**

American Revolution Declaration of Independence

Battle of Shiloh U.S. Constitution

RULE 14: **Capitalize the names of languages.**

English Spanish

Chinese French

RULE 15: **Capitalize the Roman numerals and the letters of the first major topics in an outline.**

I.
   A.
   B.

II.
   A.
   B.
   C.

Capitalize only the first word in an outline unless the words are a proper noun.

I. Oceans and seas
   A. Major oceans
   B. Major seas

II. Land forms
   A. Western hemisphere continents
      1. North America   (proper noun)
      2. South America   (proper noun)
   B. Eastern hemisphere continents

RULE 16: **Capitalize the first word of a direct quotation.**

Examples: Harley asked, "How old is your brother?"

"He is five," said Jodi.

Note: **Do not capitalize the word following the quotation unless it is a proper noun.**

274   "He looks older," said Harley.

Name_____

Date_____

Directions: Write the capital letter above any word that needs to be capitalized.

          M   C   E
    Example: The magna carta is an important document in england.

1.   some massachusetts colonists signed a document called the mayflower compact.

2.   "have you seen my magazine?" asked jackie.

3.   is english spoken in that country?

4.   "don't leave me!" shrieked the small child.

5.   i.   dogs

          a.   types

             1.   short hair

             2.   long hair

          b.   care

       ii.   cats

6.   the american revolution gave americans freedom.

7.   in canada, both french and english are spoken.

8.   judy said, "your button is open."

9.   general andrew jackson led the battle of new orleans.

10.   bo asked, "are you ready to leave?"

11.   "we will leave in fifteen minutes," vincent replied.

12.   brook's dad speaks german and russian.

Directions: Write the capital letter above any word that needs to be capitalized.

                              H

Example: "how did you do that?" asked the smiling lady.

1. i. animals

     a. those with one cell

          1. amoeba

          2. paramecium

     b. those with more than one cell

  ii. plants

2. the battle of bull run was fought during the civil war.

3. "where have you been?" asked miss posey.

4. they learned italian at their high school.

5. did thomas jefferson write the declaration of independence?

6. "you're right!" yelled mrs. frie.

7. our friend named mario speaks the spanish language.

8. the u. s. constitution is our nation's written government.

9. a weatherman said, "tomorrow's weather should be sunny."

10. did general cornwallis surrender to general washington at the battle of yorktown?

11. is the portuguese language spoken in the country of brazil?

12. the ballot was written both in english and in spanish.

RULE 17:   Capitalize brand names but not the products.

      Carnello candles   Skine computer disc

      Richy ice cream   Yummy hot dogs

RULE 18:   Capitalize religions, religious documents, names of churches, and names for a supreme being.

      Christian   (religion)   Ten Commandments   (document)

      Moslem   (religion)   <u>Bible</u>

      Heavenly Father   Palmcroft Baptist Church

      God   Talmud   (writings of the Jewish religion)

Notes:

A.   Capitalize a religious denomination such as Methodist or Baptist. If the name of a specific church is not given, capitalize only the denomination.
    Example: a Baptist church   (The name of a church is not given.)

B.   Do not capitalize the terms gods and goddesses.

RULE 19:   Capitalize a proper adjective but not the noun it modifies.

      a California beach   a Memorial Day parade

      a Payson music festival   an African nation

RULE 20:   Capitalize the first word of a greeting and closing of a letter.

      My dearest friend,   Sincerely yours,

RULE 21:   Capitalize directions when they refer to a region of a country or the world.

      Examples: Georgia is in the South.   (region of the U.S.)

            He lives in China which is also called the East.
                            (region of the world)

Name_____ **CAPITALIZATION**

Date_____

Directions: Write the capital letter above any word that needs to be capitalized.

                 T   N E
Example: they live in the new england states.

1. (H) have you visited the (W) west?

2. (C) clay's grandmother lives near a (R) rhode (I) island beach.

3. (D) dear (J) jamilla,

    (I) i just wanted to let you know that my family will be visiting the (E) east soon.

                                (Y) your friend,
                                (K) kaloni

4. (D) did (T) tama attend a (N) nogales craft show in (N) northern (M) mexico?

5. (H) has he always liked (B) bashy's spearmint gum and (C) cuddle's peanut butter cups?

6. (P) pastor (N) ngi led the service at (S) silverdale (M) methodist (C) church.

7. (M) maxim lives in (A) arizona, one of the states of the (S) southwest.

8. (T) the women attended a (C) christian conference at a (P) presbyterian church.

9. (W) were the (D) dead (S) sea (S) scrolls found in the (M) middle (E) east*?

10. (F) franco likes (P) party (P) pride hot dogs with (R) rubio's mustard and onion.

11. (T) the (B) benz family goes to the mountains each (L) labor (D) day weekend.

12. (M) many people in the country of (I) india practice the (H) hindu religion.

13. (I) is (C) chicago the largest city in the (M) midwest?

14. (H) his parents bought a (G) galaxy television from an appliance store in the (S) south.

*name of a region of the world
278

Name_____ **CAPITALIZATION**

Date_____

Directions: Write the capital letter above any word that needs to be capitalized.

Example: that school closes before memorial day weekend.
(T above that, M above memorial, D above day)

1. to my aunt, (T above to)

   thank you for taking me to the new jersey beach in july. (T above thank, N above new, J above jersey, J above july)

   your nephew, (Y above your)
   pablo (P above pablo)

2. she traveled to thailand, a country in asia. (S above she, T above thailand, A above asia)

3. a labor day parade passed northeast of their home. (A above a, L above labor, D above day, N above northeast)

4. dinner consisted of korco macaroni and cheese with dobby's peas. (D above dinner, K above korco, D above dobby's)

5. ebony attended a christian conference in the south. (E above ebony, C above christian, S above south)

6. the name of the wyoming rodeo was "old west corral time." (T above the, W above wyoming, O above old, W above west, C above corral, T above time)

7. did tomas read about greek goddesses in that book? (D above did, T above tomas, G above greek)

8. his mother visited a shinto* temple in japan. (H above his, S above shinto, J above japan)

9. seth always buys lavis jeans and hiking boots. (S above seth, L above lavis)

10. dear ara, (D above dear, A above ara)

    will you send me pictures of boise and other places you have visited in the northwest? (W above will, B above boise, N above northwest)

    your cousin, (Y above your)
    jacy (J above jacy)

11. that utah ski resort is very busy during christmas vacation. (T above that, U above utah, C above christmas)

12. have you ever eaten simpson's onion soup or richtown's tomato soup? (H above have, S above simpson's, R above richtown's)

*religion (R above religion)

279

DO NOT CAPITALIZE

RULE 1: **Do not capitalize the seasons of the year.**

        spring   summer   autumn/fall   winter

RULE 2: **Do not capitalize school subjects unless they have a number or name a language.**

We like science, spelling, social studies, geography, and history.

Patrick studies **A**lgebra II, **S**panish, and **B**iology 204 in high school.

If a proper adjective appears with the subject, capitalize only the proper adjective.
    American history   **G**reek literature

RULE 3: **Do not capitalize north, south, east, west, northeast, northwest, southeast, or southwest when they are directions.**

Go north on Ludlow Street.

Do not capitalize regions of a state, county, or city.
Are you moving to southern Texas?
Sissy lives in northeastern Anaheim.

RULE 4: **Do not capitalize career choices.**

Their dad is a teacher.
Hannah wants to be a computer programmer.

RULE 5: **Do not capitalize foods.**

    fudge   beef   apples   lemonade
    milk   tacos   lettuce   cookies

If a proper adjective appears with the food, capitalize the proper adjective but not the food.
    Swiss cheese   **G**erman pancakes

RULE 6: **Do not capitalize diseases.**

    measles   mumps   polio   chicken pox
    cancer   flu   hepatitis   arthritis

Name_____   **CAPITALIZATION REVIEW**

Date_____

Directions: Write the capital letter above any word that needs to be capitalized.

                        T   B   B   H   A   R
         Example: the battle of bunker hill was fought during the american revolution.

1.   23 horton road
                                                                      ruidoso, new mexico   88345
                                                                      september 30, 20--

         dear kissa,

                   we had a great time on our vacation to nebraska.

                                                                      your friend,
                                                                      chan

2.   uncle dakota, will you go with me to darby general store?

3.   did the axton boys choir perform at a fair in june?

4.   last spring, captain contos visited the new york museum of art.

5.   at thanksgiving, grandma kline serves sweet potatoes with a bobco* turkey.

6.   have mr. and mrs. shatler taken an arrow airlines flight to alaska?

7.   she and i attended a <u>bible</u> study at scottsdale bible church.

8.   ander attended an elementary school before going to riser high school.

9.   the arizona state fair occurs each fall in southern phoenix.

10.   was the gettysburg address written by president abraham lincoln?

11.   the people of the moslem faith read a book called the <u>koran</u>.

12.   in the summer, their uncle works at a colorado cattle ranch near denver.
*brand name

Name_____   **CAPITALIZATION REVIEW**

Date_____

Directions: Write the capital letter above any word that needs to be capitalized.

                                A   W   H
       Example: are you allowed to tour the east wing of the white house*?

1.   the gentleman was admitted to bayview hospital for bronchitis.

2.   the state of oregon is in the pacific northwest, a region of the united states.

3.   has dad collected donations for the american cancer society?

4.   the poem entitled "winter night" begins with the line, "pile high the hickory..."

5.   although kino lives in west virginia, he was born in the southwest.

6.   at mountain junior high school, nikko took science, spanish, english, and math II.

7.   does deka play the trombone for the miller county adult band?

8.   the eiffel tower in paris, france, is lighted at night.

9.   the wally workout club has a summer special in august.

10.   is the gold king hotel in irving, texas, near the airport?

11.   in american literature class, mario and amber read <u>the red badge of courage</u>.

12.   if you go to pike's peak, you will be near colorado springs.

13.   is monticello, the name of thomas jefferson's home, on the potomac river?

14.   i.   beach activities
          a.   volleyball
          b.   surfing
      ii.   camping activities
          a.   hiking
          b.   mountain bike riding

*home of the United States President

286

PUNCTUATION

PERIOD: (.)

RULE 1:   **Use a period at the end of a declarative sentence (statement).**

    We found a bird that had fallen from its nest.

RULE 2:   **Place a period at the end of an imperative sentence (command).**

    Please take this with you.

RULE 3:   **Use a period after initial(s).**

    Jeremy **J.** Wing is my friend.

RULE 4:   **Use a period after the letter(s) and number(s) in an outline.**

    I. Birds
       A. Birds that fly
       B. Birds that don't fly
          1. Penguins
          2. Ostriches
   II. Reptiles
       A. Poisonous
       B. Non-poisonous

RULE 5:   **Place a period after an abbreviation.**

    A.   **Days of the week:**

Sunday- Sun.	Thursday - Thurs., Thur.*
Monday - Mon.	Friday - Fri.
Tuesday - Tues., Tue.*	Saturday - Sat.
Wednesday- Wed.	*The first listing is preferred.

    B.   **Months of the year:**

January - Jan.	July
February - Feb.	August - Aug.
March - Mar.	September - Sept.
April - Apr.	October - Oct.
May	November - Nov.
June	December - Dec.

    C.   **Times:**

A.M. - Latin ante meridiem	(before noon)
P.M. - Latin post meridiem	(after noon)

D.   Directions:

N. - north   S. - south   E. - east   W. - west

E.   Titles:

Mrs. - title used before a married woman's name (plural = Mmes.)
Mr. - Mister
Ms. - title that doesn't show if a woman is married or unmarried
Dr. - Doctor
Gen. - General
Capt. - Captain
Sen. - Senator

F.   Places (general):

Ave. - Avenue   Blvd. - Boulevard
Ln. - Lane   Hwy. - Highway
St. - Street (or Saint)   Mt. - Mountain (Mts. - Mountains)
Dr. - Drive   Str. - Strait
Always use a dictionary to check for proper abbreviations.

G: Places (Specific):

Mt. Rushmore - Mount Rushmore   SD - South Dakota*
Ft. Lauderdale - Fort Lauderdale   Penna. - Pennsylvania
St. Augustine - Saint Augustine   (*Using the two letter postal
U.S.A. - United States of America   code for each states is sug-
Eur. - Europe   gested; no periods are used.)

H.   Associations and Organizations:

Y.W.C.A. - Young Women's Christian Association
Y.M.H.A. - Young Men's Hebrew Association

If the dictionary provides two possibilities, the first given is preferred.

A.M.A. - American Medical Association
E.M.A. - Entrepreneurial Mothers' Association
Madd - Mothers Against Drunk Drivers*
NOW - National Organization of Women*

*If the initials spell out a word, the word is called an acronym. **Do not use periods with acronyms.**

I.   Other abbreviations:

MP - Military Police (also M.P.)   Mgr. - Manager
Co. - Company   Assn. - Association

If a declarative sentence ends with a period, do not place an additional period.
Example: Julius Caesar died in 44 B.C.

Name_____

Date_____

Directions: Place a period where needed.

1.   Mr Harmon wants to drive that car

2.   Capt Stelwell will meet with us this Thurs at two o'clock

3.   Give your paper about the meeting in Aug to Miss Fields

4.   King Tutankhamen lived about 1355 B C in Egypt

5.   Milly D Rivers lives at 12 E Oak Street

6.   I Presidents

        A   Abraham Lincoln

        B   John Kennedy

        C   George Bush

     II Famous wives of Presidents

        A   Abigail Adams

        B   Bess Truman

7.   They will meet at the Chrysler Bldg at 9 A M

8.   Has Dr Blair J Adams gone to the A M A meeting?

9.   Their new address is 453 N Ashton, St Louis, MO 63367

10.   On Sat , Oct 9th, a fashion show was held by the club

11.   Sen H Lipton has lived in the U S all of his life

Apostrophe: (')

Rule 1: **Use an apostrophe in a contraction to show where a letter or letters have been omitted.**

> doesn't = does not
> we're = we are
> what's = what is

Rule 2: **Use an apostrophe when the first two digits are omitted from the year.**

> '87 = 1987
> '98 = 1998
> '11 = 2011

Rule 3: **Use an apostrophe when referring to letters or words used out of context.**

> Be sure to dot your i's.
> The a in your and's needs to be closed.

Rule 4: **Use an apostrophe to show possession (ownership):**

A. **If the word is singular (one), add apostrophe + s.**

> a house's roof
> one lady's shoes
> the teller's smile

B. **If the word is plural (more than one) and ends in s, add the apostrophe after the s.**

> two girls' room
> several babies' toy
> many students' projects

C. **If the word is plural (more than one) and does not end in s, add apostrophe + s.**

> men's restroom
> mice's tails
> children's petting zoo

Note: When two people own the same item, add an apostrophe + s after the **second** name.   Bob and Jan**'s** new home   (They own a home together.)
When two people own separate items, add an apostrophe + s after **both** names.   Tom**'s** and Sue**'s** basketballs   (They each have a basketball.)

290

Name_____   **APOSTROPHES**

Date_____

Directions: Write the possessive.

Example: skis belonging to her mother: ___her mother's skis___

1.   a ferret belonging to Fred: _____

2.   boots belonging to their dad: _____

3.   a horse belonging to Chris: _____

4.   golf clubs belonging to Miss Hand: _____

5.   a restaurant owned by two men: _____

6.   a trampoline belonging to three girls: _____

7.   a work area belonging to several teachers: _____

8.   a trail for many walkers: _____

9.   a club formed by several boys: _____

10.   a park where five geese live: _____

11.   a balloon belonging to a child: _____

12.   the grandfather of Bess: _____

Date_____

Directions: Insert any apostrophe where needed.

     Example: She was born in '87.

1.   Lindas mother walks five miles each day.

2.   His answers werent correct.

3.   Whos going to Beverlys house?

4.   Cross your <u>ts</u>, please.

5.   We arent finished with Jackies coat.

6.   Your <u>3s</u> look more like <u>8s</u>.

7.   That nurses station is very busy.

8.   Youre invited to a childrens play.

9.   One persons luggage hadnt been found.

10.   Dot your <u>is</u> in your name.

11.   Was John F. Kennedys burial in 63?

12.   Theyve learned much about oxens habits.

13.   Weve decided to take our two aunts advice.

14.   The artists convention wasnt held in San Francisco.

15.   In 93, Mikes parents went to Denmark.

16.   Two puppies dish had been turned over.

17.   The childs grandparents arent able to attend.

18.   Your <u>6s</u> look too much like <u>9s</u>.

Comma: (,)

Rule 1:   **Place a comma after the day and year in a date.**

April 1, 1987
↟

Place a comma after the day and the date.

Sunday, September 19, 1993
↟   ↟

Place a comma after the date if the date doesn't end a sentence.

On Oct. 23, 1946, his father was born.
↟   ↟

Rule 2:   **Place a comma between a town or city and a state.**

Reno, Nevada
↟

Place a comma between a city and a country.

Paris, France
↟

In a street address, place a comma after the street and after the city. Do not place a comma between the state and zip code.

They live at 40 Flower Lane, Leeds, AL 35094.
↟   ↟

Note that a comma is not placed between the house address and the street address!

Place a comma after the state or country if it appears before the end of the sentence.

Joanna and Paul go to Racine, Wisconsin, for the summer.
↟   ↟

Rule 3:   **Use a comma to set off introductory words.**

No, I can't do that.
↟

Yes, this is the best stew ever.
↟

Well, let's decide together.

t

Rule 4: **Use a comma to set off interrupters in a sentence.**
(An interrupter usually can be removed from a sentence without changing its meaning.)

His name, by the way, is French.

t   t

The cab driver, however, must be paid immediately.

t   t

That tie, I believe, is a silk one.

t   t

Rule 5: **Place a comma after the greeting of a friendly letter**.

Dear Uncle Lloyd,

t

Place a comma after the closing of any letter.

Sincerely yours,
Chelsea   **t**

Rule 6: **Place a comma after three or more items in a series**.

A toothbrush, toothpaste, and mouthwash had been packed.

t   t

Do not place a comma after the last item in a series.

Place a comma after phrases in a series.

Miss Harper threw her head back, coughed gently, and began to laugh.

t   t

Rule 7: **Place a comma after a noun of direct address** (a person spoken to).

Cynthia, will you explain this puzzle to me?

t

I need your help, Dad.

t

Have you, Betty, seen my notebook?

t   t

294

Semicolon (;)

Rule 1: **Use a semicolon to join two complete sentences that are closely related.**

Hail began to fall; everyone ran into the building.

                    t

complete   **complete**
sentence   **sentence**

Colon (:):

Rule 1: **Use a colon in writing the time.**

5:00 P.M.   11:23 A.M.
  t   **t**

Rule 2: **Use a colon to set off lists.**

Things to take:
         t

    shoes
    socks
    shorts

We need the following: paper plates, plastic forks, and cups.
                  t

Rule 3: **Use a colon after divisions of topics in a writing.**

PLANTS:
     t
Land plants:
        t

Rule 4: **Place a colon after the greeting of a business letter.**

Dear Sir: Ladies and Gentlemen:
  t   **t**

Date_____

Directions: Insert needed semicolons and colons.

1.   Dear Sir

2.   The football game will begin at 7 30 A.M.

3.   Things to do
      -wash car
      -feed dog
      -take out trash

4.   Rule A   Take turns.

     Rule B   Be polite.

5.   Homework was given in the following subjects   math, English, and spelling.

6.   The cake is cherry   the frosting is cream cheese.

7.   Your appointment is at 5 15 or 5 30.

8.   Dear Senator Sung

9.   Let's shop at 6 30 for the following napkins, balloons, and party horns.

10.   Her hair is very curly someone must have given her a perm.

11.   You may go on these days Monday, Wednesday, Thursday, and Saturday.

12.   Carlo's mother answered the phone she called for Carlo to come.

13.   People going on the trip
       -Micah
       -Laylah
       -Jina

14.   To whom it may concern

Question Mark (?):

Rule 1: Use a question mark at the end of an interrogative sentence. (An interrogative sentence asks a question.)

> Is Cape Cod in Massachusetts?
> May I bring my belongings?

Exclamation Point (!):

Rule 1: Use an exclamation point after an exclamatory sentence. (An exclamatory sentence shows strong feeling.)

> We've been chosen!
> Our team is ahead by two points!

Rule 2: Place an exclamation point after a word or phrase that shows strong feeling (interjection).

> Wow!   Yippee! We did it!

Hyphen (-):

Rule 1: Place a hyphen between fractions and two digit word numbers between 21 and 99.

> four-fifths   one-half   twenty-two   seventy-eight
>   ↟   ↟   ↟   ↟

Rule 2: Use a hyphen to combine some prefixes with a root word.

> self-concept   ex-president
>   ↟   ↟

Use a dictionary to determine if words should be hyphenated.

Rule 3: Use a hyphen to combine some closely related words.

> see-through   three-speed
>   ↟   ↟

Use a dictionary to determine if words should be hyphenated.

Rule 4: Use a hyphen when dividing a word of two or more syllables at the end of a line. (Words are divided between syllables.) You must have at least *two* letters on the first line and *three* on the following line.

Check a dictionary if you are not sure where to divide a word.

	re-
fund	
	jel-
lyfish	
	divi-
sion	

Incorrect:
	a-	(Two or more letters are required.)
bout		
	quick-	
ly		(Three or more letters are required.)

Underlining ( ):

Rule 1: **Underline the names of ships, planes, and trains.**
Spruce Goose (name of an airplane)
Princess (name of a ship)
Oriental Express (name of a train)

Rule 2: **Underline letter(s), word(s), or number(s) used out of context.**
Please cross your t.
I used too four times in this paragraph.
Your 3's are too small.

Rule 3: **Underline the title of books, magazines, movies, newspapers, plays, television shows, and record albums/CD's/tapes, works of art, sculptures, operas, and long poems.**
Note: An item is usually underlined if you can receive it in the mail.
Scripts for plays and television shows are long and follow this rule.

Have you read a recent issue of Ranger Rick? (magazine)
He read the book, Old Yeller, and saw the movie, 101 Dalmations.
USA Today is an interesting newspaper.
She wrote a play entitled George Washington and the French.
The child watched a re-run of Mr. Rogers on television.
The tape, In His Time, is very enjoyable.

302 **Note: In print, a title will be in italics rather than underlined.**

Name_____

Date_____

**QUESTION MARKS
EXCLAMATION POINTS
HYPHENS
UNDERLINING**

Directions: Insert needed punctuation (question marks, exclamation points, hyphens, and underlinings).

Example: Mr. Lampner just bought a ten-speed bike.

1.   Hurrah   I found my money

2.   Two thirds of the flowers have been planted; however, most of the daf fodils are still in cartons.

3.   Will you please choose a seat

4.   The Queen Mary* is in Long Beach, California.

     *name of a ship

5.   The Mertz family bought a tri level home.

6.   Thirty four people waited in line.

7.   Lulu's mom read the book, Boost Your Brainpower.

8.   Mrs. Haas added three fourths cup of honey to the cookie recipe.

9.   Lana buys a copy of Pretty Parties* each month.

     *name of a magazine

10.   The teacher wrote a gigantic 9 on the board.

11.   The woman on the subway was reading The Money Market Journal*.

     *name of a newspaper

12.   The movie, Gone with the Wind, is very long.

13.   The man paced to and fro in the lobby.

14.   Be sure to dot you i and cross your t's in the word mitten.

15.   Oh The fireworks during the half time celebration were terrific.

<u>**Quotation Marks (" "):**</u>

Rule 1: **Use quotation marks (" ") to indicate someone's exact words.**

"How are you?" asked Miss Dow.
Danny said, "I am fine."

    A. **In a split quotation, place quotations around each part spoken.**

"Your knee," said Mrs. Lincoln, "looks very sore."
"It is sore," said Tom. "I fell and skinned it."

    B. **In a split quotation, do not place the end quotation mark until the person has finished speaking.**

"Let's try," said Jimmie, "Take my hand. Now pull hard on the rope."

    C. **In dialogue (conversation between two or more people), begin a new paragraph each time a different person speaks.**

Roberta asked, "Tom, have you seen the little puppy that I just received for my birthday?"
"What kind is he?" Tom asked.
"He's a cocker spaniel," replied Roberta.
"Would you like to go to my house to show my parents?" asked Tom.

Rule 2: **Use quotation marks to enclose the title of short poems, short stories, nursery rhymes, songs, chapters, articles, and essays.**

Note: **Periods and commas are always placed inside quotation marks. Other punctuation is placed outside unless it is included in the actual question.**

He read the poem, "Stopping by Woods on a Snowy Evening."
The newspaper article was entitled "Club to Meet."
"Why Mosquitoes Buzz in People's Ears" is the first story they read.
Is their favorite nursery rhyme "Wee Willie Winkle"?
The fifth chapter in the history book is "The Pioneers."
Grandmother's favorite song is "In the Garden."
Nan's essay entitled "Doughboys" is about World War I.

Note: ***Any "item" that is contained within a larger one is usually placed in quotation marks.*** For example: A magazine article is in a magazine.

                              Chapters are within a book.

Directions: Insert needed quotation marks.

1. Let's play together,   said Bruce.

2. Molly shouted, Come here!

3. The first chapter of that history book is entitled Native Americans.

4. Mrs. Claire Little said,   Ladies, we are here to discuss the new library.

5. Have you read the poem entitled The Sands of Dee ?

6. Give me your hand, said the mother to the child.

7. They listened to the song, Good Vibrations.

8. Your facts, said the manager, are correct.

9. The children read a short story entitled The Rescue at Sea.

10. Have you memorized the nursery rhyme, Old Mother Hubbard ?

11. I know,   said the mother,   that you aren't finished. However, it's time for supper.

12. David's essay entitled Colonial America won a prize.

13. The magazine article was entitled Travels in China.

14. How,   asked the lost driver, do I get to Dover Drive?

15. Write a dialogue between two people:

    _____

    _____

    _____

    _____

    _____   305

Name_____

Date_____

Directions: Place quotation marks or underline the following titles:

1. a song, Red River Valley

2. a book, Herbs

3.   a magazine, Scuba News

4. a magazine article, Down the Mississippi River

5. a video tape, Amazon: Land of the Flooded Forest

6.   a short story, Buffalo Bill

7.   a short poem, I Came to the New World

8.   a ship, Titanic

9. an airplane, Air King

10. a work of art, Woman with a Child

11.   a nursery rhyme, Hickory Dickory Dock

12.   a newspaper, Tri-City Tribune

13.   a movie, The Rescuers

14.   a magazine article, The Perfect Diet

15.   an album, Love

16.   a play, Columbus

17.   an essay, Why I Believe in America

18.   a television show, Sports

19.   a newspaper article, Suspect Held in Burglary

20.   a chapter, Animals of the Desert

306

Name_____ **PUNCTUATION REVIEW**

Date_____

Directions: Insert needed punctuation.

1. Yes my mother is home

2. His mother and father read the Midwest Times*
       *name of a newspaper

3. Dino come here

4. Fifty nine people boarded a run down bus

5. He was born on Jan 1 1984

6. Almira said   Let me help you

7. Their address is 20874 N Briar Road

8. I will call you and we will plan a party

9. They saw Bear Country at the 9 30 P M movie

10. Groceries
        -eggs
        -milk
        -bread

11. Your father I believe is looking for you

12. Jinas story is called The Two Huge Pandas

13. A girls club was formed by Lollie her sister and her cousin

14. Gentlemen

        The meeting will be held at 10 30 A M in the conference room of the Hor
    ton Hotel

                                        Sincerely
                                        William T Cortez

15. Mona likes to read Royal British magazine

Name_____

Date_____

Directions: Insert needed punctuation.

1.   Youre my pal Tate

2.   Abram asked May I speak with you

3.   Mrs E Babbit is the childrens librarian

4.   A fat chewy brownie is on the plate

5.   At 3 15 P M Chandas game will begin

6.   Mr Blake drives a two tone car

7.   Dinah read Little Miss Muffet* to her little brother
        *name of a nursery rhyme

8.   Wheres my glove asked Marcus

9.   Their new address is 22 Roe Road Mandeville LA 70448

10.   Dear Michelle

        Were going to Norman Oklahoma

                            Your friend
                            Kimo

11.   Ouch I smashed my finger

12.   Janell Aleta and I did the laundry

13.   Take the umbrella youll need it if it rains

14.   The ladies church group discussed the book entitled The Prayer of Jabez

15.   Roxanne asked Have you pulled the weeds in the garden

Date_____

Directions: Insert needed punctuation.

1. To do list
    -feed dog
    -bathe dog
    -wash dogs dish

2. On Nov 2 1999 Jim and Lois plan to marry

3. Chip our beagle is short and stout

4. Have you read the book entitled Angels

5. You are using too many ands in your writing

6. Three fifths of Greggs baseball cards are valuable

7. Miss Adams wants the following a bike a chain and a lock

8. Whose is this asked Gen Morton

9. Thirty seven cheerleaders traveled to Richmond Virginia for a meeting

10. Youll enjoy reading the article entitled Exercise Daily in that magazine

11. I want said Capt Bing to visit Yellowstone soon

12. On Thursday Oct 21 she will be twenty one

13. No he wont travel to London England in the fall

14. We can sled ski or play in the snow but it will be very cold

15. Write a friend's name in inverted form: _____

16. This dish said the elderly lady belonged to my grandmother

IMPORTANT WORDS

THERE, THEIR, THEY'RE:

1. **There is an adverb meaning where.**

   Examples: Have you gone **there**?

   There are five airplanes ready to take off.

2. **Their is a pronoun that shows possession.** When using *their*, you should be able to answer *"their what?"*

   Example: She sang at **their** wedding.   (Their what? wedding)

3. **They're is a contraction meaning they are.** If you think *they're* should be used, read the sentence inserting *they are*.

   Examples: **RIGHT: They're** leaving in the morning.
   They are leaving in the morning.

   WRONG: Is this **they're** car?
   Is this they are car?

🐢 🐢 🐢 🐢 🐢 🐢 🐢 🐢 🐢 🐢 🐢 🐢 🐢 🐢 🐢 🐢 🐢 🐢 🐢 🐢

MAY or CAN?:

1. A. **May asks permission.**

   Example: **May** I eat dinner now?
   (asking permission)

   B.   **May also suggests a possibility.**

   Example: I **may** return earlier.

2. **Can means that one is able to do something.**

   Example: **Can** you fix this?
   (Are you able to fix this?)

310

NOTES

Name_____

Date_____

A **semicolon** is a comma with a period above it **(;)**.

A semicolon may be used to join two complete thoughts. That means that each thought must be able to stand alone as a **complete sentence**.

It's important to know if the group of words expresses a complete thought.

Examples: Ponderosa pines are tall.   **(complete thought)**
                                                   (sentence)

Rafe and Jude in the afternoon. **(not a complete thought)**
Where's the verb?

If you are going with us. **(not a complete thought)**

The sentence contains a **subject** (you) and a **verb** (are going), but it does not express a complete thought.

க்கௌக்கௌக்கௌக்கௌக்கௌக்கௌ

Directions: Write **S** in the blank if the group of words is a sentence (complete thought). Write **NS** in the blank if the group of words is not a sentence (not a complete thought).

1. _____   A has been built near the center of that town.

2. _____   A stream runs along the edge of their property.

3. _____   When the football game ended.

4. _____   The tall woman owns an office supply store.

5. _____   Cutting his fingernails.

6. _____   Toasting marshmallows over an open flame.

7. _____   Before leaving for the airport.

8. _____   If you save your money.

9. _____   Nate often with his uncle and dad.

10. _____   Resting while hiking is usually a good idea.

Name_____

Date_____

A **semicolon** is a comma with a period above it **(;)**.

A semicolon may be used to join two complete thoughts. That means that each thought must be able to stand alone as a **complete sentence**.

It's important to know if the group of words expresses a complete thought.

Example: We have not seen Ty for two months. (**complete thought**)
(**sentence**)

Stop! (**complete thought - sentence**)

 Look at this one-word sentence carefully. It is an imperative sentence (command). The subject is (You) — *you understood*. Always read a group of words carefully. A sentence can be just one word (especially in a command) or many words.

Traveling in a four-wheel vehicle. (**not a complete thought**)

After we finish this lesson. (**not a complete thought**)

The sentence contains a ***subject*** (we) and a ***verb*** (finish), but it does not express a complete thought. We don't know what will happen after the lesson.

ॐॐॐॐॐॐॐॐॐॐॐ

Directions: Write **S** in the blank if the group of words is a sentence (complete thought). Write **NS** in the blank if the group of words is not a sentence (not a complete thought).

1. _____ She did a recent study of the stock market.

2. _____ Jump.

3. _____ When a child loses his first tooth.

4. _____ The pony with a golden mane and tail in the meadow.

5. _____ Go to the end of the hallway and turn right.

6. _____ Throughout the first days of kindergarten with his new teacher.

7. _____ His family never goes to underground caverns.

A semicolon is a comma with a period above it (;). It joins two complete thoughts.

    1st complete thought (sentence):   The man shoveled all day.
    2nd complete thought (sentence):   A blister formed on his palm.

      Example: A man shoveled all day; a blister formed on his palm.

The two thoughts must be about the same topic!

      Wrong: The man shoveled all day; he is going to Bermuda next year.
      Right: The man shoveled all day; a blister formed on his palm.

Sometimes, words such as *however* or *therefore* will follow the semicolon. Place a comma after *however* or *therefore.*

   Example: The man shoveled all day; ***therefore,*** a blister formed on his palm.

                ʘ ʘ ʘ ʘ ʘ ʘ ʘ ʘ ʘ ʘ ʘ ʘ

Directions: Use a semicolon where needed.

1. Their sister is a lawyer their brother owns a cleaning service.

2. This steak is very tough therefore, I can't eat it.

3. Sit with us this chair is not saved.

4. Frances Perkins became the Secretary of Labor in 1933 she was the first female member of a Cabinet.

5. Renoir was a famous artist however, he started by painting china.

6. New race cars are expensive therefore, they will look for a used one.

7. The Netherlands once had 10,000 windmills however, only 1,000 remain.

8. A persimmon is plum-like however, it is orange-red in color, not purple.

9. Ford auto workers earned $5 a day in 1914 that was an excellent wage then.
324

A semicolon is a comma with a period above it (;). It joins two complete thoughts.

    1st complete thought (sentence):   Jane's answer was fifty-two.
    2nd complete thought (sentence):   It was wrong.

    Example: Jane's answer was fifty-two; it was wrong.

The two thoughts must be about the same topic!

    Wrong: Jane's answer was fifty-two; her aunt lives on Lynx Lane.
    Right: Jane's answer was fifty-two; it was wrong.

Sometimes, words such as *however, therefore, fortunately,* or *unfortunately* or phrases like *in fact* will follow a semicolon. Place a comma after these words or phrases.

    Example: Jane's answer was fifty-two; ***unfortunately,*** it was wrong.

ଽଈଽଈଽଈଽଈଽଈଽଈଽଈଽଈଽଈଽଈ

Directions: Use a semicolon where needed.

1. I had to be at the airport by 6 o'clock fortunately, I woke at 4.

2. Jerry wanted to become a cowboy when he was little however, he became a congressman.

3. The Dead Sea Scrolls were found in a cave they were in stone jars.

4. Jackie Robinson was the first Black to be hired as a professional baseball player he had been an All American halfback at the University of California.

5. Everyone wanted pizza unfortunately, no one had money.

6. Mika won the school's spelling bee in fact, she went on to win the state one.

7. Margaret Thatcher became prime minister of England in 1979 however, she had been educated at Oxford University as a chemist and a lawyer.

8. Our dishwasher has broken therefore, we need to buy a new one.

A semicolon is a comma with a period above it (;). It joins two complete thoughts.   The two thoughts must be about the <u>same</u> topic!

Sometimes, *however, therefore, fortunately, unfortunately,* or *in fact* will follow a semicolon. Place a **comma** after them.

      Example: We waded in a shallow stream; ***fortunately***, it was clear and clean.

               ᜆᜆᜆᜆᜆᜆᜆᜆᜆᜆᜆᜆ

Directions: The first complete thought has been written for you. Place a semicolon and finish the sentence.

<u>**Remember**</u>: **You can use *however, therefore, fortunately, unfortunately, or in fact* if it makes sense. Don't forget the comma after these words.**

1.   Alaska became the forty-ninth state in 1959 _____

_____

2.   Miss Jaco teaches us math _____

_____

3.   Todd won first prize in a cooking contest _____

_____

4.   John F. Kennedy became President of the United States in 1960 _____

_____

5. The jury found the woman innocent _____

_____

326

A semicolon is a comma with a period above it (;). It joins two complete thoughts.   The two thoughts must be about the <u>same</u> topic!

Sometimes, *however, therefore, fortunately, unfortunately,* or *in fact* will follow a semicolon. Place a **comma** after them.

      Example: Santa Fe is a city in New Mexico; ***in fact,*** it is the state capital.

                          ৰ৵ৰ৵ৰ৵ৰ৵ৰ৵ৰ৵ৰ৵ৰ৵ৰ৵ৰ৵ৰ৵

Directions: The first complete thought has been written for you. Place a
                     semicolon and finish the sentence.

<u>Remember:</u>   **You can use *however, therefore, fortunately, unfortunately,* or *in fact*
                   if it makes sense. Don't forget the comma after these words.**

1. <u>Cindy handed a clerk her credit card</u>_____

    _____

2. <u>Dad is being transferred to Tulsa</u>_____

    _____

3. <u>The television show, *Sesame Street*, began in 1969</u>_____

    _____

4. <u>Joey and Lulu collect baseball cards</u>_____

    _____

5. <u>A hurricane hit the area</u>_____

    _____

NOTES

In order to understand compound sentences, we need to review *complete thoughts*.

Examples: The children slept in a tent in the backyard.   (**complete thought**)

After they went to bed. (**not a complete thought**)

The sentence contains a ***subject*** (they) and a ***verb*** (went), but it does not express a complete thought. More information is needed.

A compound sentence is formed by joining **two complete thoughts** with ***and, but,*** or ***or.***

Kiki is our new kitten, ***and*** we named our puppy Ginger.

complete thought   complete thought

This clock doesn't work, ***but*** his mother can repair it.

complete thought   complete thought

Directions: Write **S** in the blank if the group of words is a sentence (complete thought). Write **NS** in the blank if the group of words is not a sentence (not a complete thought).

1. _____   By the time we arrived.
2. _____   Broth was used to make this soup.
3. _____   Another senator was elected.
4. _____   Unless you begin immediately.
5. _____   The boy with his arms crossed and smiling.
6. _____   As you step over the puddle.
7. _____   After we reached the top of the hill.
8. _____   Because the car wash was closed.
9. _____   After school, we may go to the zoo.

In order to understand compound sentences, we need to review *complete thoughts*.

Examples: Malaria is a disease that causes a fever.   (**complete thought**)

Wait! (**complete thought**)
This is an imperative sentence; it gives a command and is a complete thought. The subject of this sentence is (You), you understood.

When Dr. Hare retires. (**not a complete thought**)

The sentence contains a ***subject*** (Dr. Hare) and a ***verb*** (retires), but it does not express a complete thought. More information is needed.

A compound sentence is formed by joining **two complete thoughts** with ***and***, ***but***, or ***or***.

The two ladies laid tile, ***and*** their husbands removed wallpaper.

complete thought   *complete thought*

Jodi has to take another course, ***or*** she won't graduate in June.

complete thought   *complete thought*

Directions: Write **S** in the blank if the group of words is a sentence (complete thought.) Write **NS** in the blank if the group of words is not a sentence (not a complete thought).

1. _____   Push on the door.

2. _____   After we counted our money.

3. _____   Jana will be traveling to Japan next week.

4. _____   Although we have never met our great uncle.

5. _____   Until your grades improve.

6. _____   When my mother was a teenager.

7. _____   The artist's hands are smudged with paint.

A compound sentence is formed by joining **two complete thoughts** with *and*, *but*, or *or*.

Place a **comma before a conjunction** when it is joining two complete thoughts.

    Example: Royce wrote a poem**,** but he didn't share it.
                 complete thought   **complete thought**

              ☙☙☙☙☙☙☙☙☙☙☙☙

Directions: Write a conjunction and another complete thought to finish each compound sentence. Be sure to place a comma before the conjunction.

1.   They planted a garden _____

     _____

2.   One presenter arrived at her seminar late _____

     _____

3.   Phoenix, Arizona, is a pretty city _____

     _____

4.   You may place a stamp on your envelope _____

     _____

5.   Our governor will not run next term _____

     _____

6.   *Mary Poppins* was a popular movie in 1964 _____

     _____

A compound sentence is formed by joining **two complete thoughts** with *and*, *but*, or *or*.

Place a **comma before a conjunction** when it is joining two complete thoughts.

Example: Mona diced onions, but her eyes began to sting.
            complete thought   **complete thought**

ᢟᢟᢟᢟᢟᢟᢟᢟᢟᢟᢟᢟ

Directions: Write a conjunction and another complete thought to finish each compound sentence. Be sure to place a comma before the conjunction.

1. Callie needs to buy a new computer _____

   _____

2. Thomas Jefferson was our third president _____

   _____

3. We wanted to buy popcorn at the theater _____

   _____

4. Their new baby sister only weighs five pounds _____

   _____

5. Many of the passengers stood in line for the flight _____

   _____

6. Pedro has earned a scholarship to Yale _____

   _____

NOTES

A clause has a subject and a verb.

> **Remember:** The subject tells *who* or *what* the sentence is "about."
> The verb tells *what is (was)* or *what happens (happened)*.
>
> <u>Mike</u> and his <u>dog</u> <u>use</u> this trail.

A clause that can stand alone as a **compete sentence** is called an **independent clause.**

> *Mike and his dog use this trail.* **=** independent clause
> **complete thought**

Sometimes, a clause cannot stand alone. An incomplete thought is called a **dependent clause**.

> After <u>we</u> <u>went</u> to our friend's house **=** dependent clause
> **incomplete thought**

<u>**This is a clause.**</u> **The subject is *we*; the verb is *went*. However, it does NOT express a**

complete thought. Therefore, it is a dependent clause.

🙡🙡🙡🙡🙡🙡🙡🙡🙡🙡🙡

Directions: Read each clause. Write <u>**DC**</u> if the clause is a dependent clause;
write <u>**IC**</u> if the clause is an independent clause and can stand alone.

1. _____   Before snow drifted on the roads.

2. _____   While we were grocery shopping.

3. _____   Her blonde hair turned green from the chlorine in the pool.

4. _____   Unless you must stop for a short break.

5. _____   If the price is right.

6. _____   Have you seen a woodpecker?

7. _____   Although several people volunteered to help at the school fair.

8. _____   He needs complete silence to study.

9. _____   Whenever we watch our friend play softball.

10. _____   The tunnel may be completed by early November.

11. _____   Even though Franklin Roosevelt was related to Teddy Roosevelt.

12. _____   I must sketch a design of a car for the next century.

13. _____   As we finished placing dishes in the dishwasher.

14. _____   During the baseball game, we ate hot dogs.

15. _____   After we lay on the mattress at the furniture store last Saturday.

16. _____   In the 1950's, hula hoops became very popular.

17. _____   A geyser gushed water into the air.

18. _____   When we trim the bushes and mow the lawn.

A clause has a subject and a verb.

A clause that can stand alone as a **compete sentence** is called an **independent clause.**

> *Oak leaves begin to change colors in the fall.* **=** independent clause
> **complete thought**

Remember that **imperative sentences (commands)** may be short. The subject of an imperative sentence is (You), *you understood.*

స్త్రోస్త్రోస్త్రో

Sometimes, a clause cannot stand alone. An incomplete thought is called a **dependent clause**.

> Unless our <u>team</u> <u>rows</u> faster **=** dependent clause
> **incomplete thought**

This is a <u>clause</u>. The subject is *team*; the verb is *rows*. However, it does NOT express a complete thought. Therefore, it is a dependent clause.

స్త్రోస్త్రోస్త్రోస్త్రోస్త్రోస్త్రోస్త్రోస్త్రోస్త్రోస్త్రో

Directions: Read each clause. Write **<u>DC</u>** if the clause is a dependent clause; write **<u>IC</u>** if the clause is an independent clause and can stand alone.

1. _____   Because the battery was dead.

2. _____   Listen.

3. _____   The toddler's cake was in the shape of a teddy bear.

4. _____   Lars refused to answer the telephone.

5. _____   Whenever Mrs. Jones works late.

336

6. _____   If we receive an email.

7. _____   As she made her way to the front of the room.

8. _____   A hackberry is a black fruit.

9. _____   Because the heel has come loose from her shoe.

10. _____   Until the freeway has been completed.

11. _____   Their ministry has collected socks for small children.

12. _____   Smile.

13. _____   If I sit.

14. _____   After the President spoke to the American people.

15. _____   Always wash your hands before handling food.

16. _____   The planet Saturn has rings within rings.

17. _____   Even though the principal was absent.

18. _____   Jason met his wife at a church picnic.

19. _____   They went to their basement during a tornado alert.

20. _____   Before Hawaii became the fiftieth state.

A **clause** contains a subject and a verb.

An *independent clause* functions as a complete thought. It can stand alone as a sentence.

A *dependent clause* cannot stand alone as a complete thought.

Some sentences have **both** a dependent clause and an independent clause.

> When the tiny baby cried, his mother fed him and sang to him.
>
> **dependent clause**   **independent clause**

In this type of sentence structure, the independent clause is also called the main clause.

> When the tiny baby cried, his mother fed him and sang to him.
>
> **dependent clause**   **main clause**

Note that a comma is placed after the dependent clause when it appears at the **beginning** of the sentence.

> Before we went to a movie, we met at Micah's house.
>
> **dependent clause**   **independent clause**

ॐ ॐ ॐ ॐ ॐ ॐ ॐ ॐ ॐ ॐ ॐ

Directions: In each sentence, read the dependent clause. Write an appropriate main (independent) clause. Be sure to place a comma at the end of the dependent clause.

Example: <u>Unless you speak up**, I can't hear you.**</u>

1.   <u>After you finish dinner_____</u>

   _____

2.   While I was walking to my friend's house _____

_____

3.   When his sister becomes angry _____

_____

4.   If you want my help _____

_____

5.   Before I go to bed _____

_____

6.   Whenever I am sick _____

_____

7.   Because his dog was barking _____

_____

8.   Although the bride had not started down the aisle _____

_____

9.   Until they went on their first vacation _____

_____

10.   If you want to go with me _____

_____

A **clause** contains a subject and a verb.

An *independent clause* functions as a complete thought. It can stand alone as a sentence.

A *dependent clause* cannot stand alone as a complete thought.

Some sentences have **both** a dependent clause and an independent clause.

Before you leave for your game**,** write a note to your dad.

dependent clause   **independent clause**

In this type of sentence structure, the independent clause is **also called** the **main clause**.

Before you leave for your game**,** write a note to your dad.

dependent clause   **main clause**

Note that a comma is placed after the dependent clause when it appears at the **beginning** of the sentence.

Do not place a comma if the dependent clause appears at the end of a sentence.

Write a note to your dad before you leave for your game.
independent clause   **dependent clause**
                (NO COMMA)

🐦🐦🐦🐦🐦🐦🐦🐦🐦🐦🐦

Directions: Read the dependent clause in each sentence. Write an appropriate main (independent) clause.

Example: Before you give your speech, **go over the key points.**

1.   When I have a sore throat_____

_____

2.   Even though Tara is very tiny

3.   After the club held a fundraiser

4.   Because his cell phone is dead

5.   Whenever the boss arrives

6.   Before Dad leaves for work

7.   Unless his bicycle is fixed

8.   If it rains tomorrow

9.   Although the first-grader was lively

10.   While a hair stylist cut her hair

NOTES

One type of participial phrase is made using the present participle of the verb.

The present participle is formed by adding **ing** to a verb.

Examples: to rise - **rising**

to grab - **grabbing**

to wish - **wishing**

Directions: Write the present participle of each verb.

1. to find _____

2. to rush _____

3. to tape _____

4. to sit _____

5. to talk _____

6. to miss _____

7. to drive _____

8. to press _____

9. to doubt _____

10. to spread _____

11. to fry _____

12. to stamp _____

13. to paint _____

14. to reach _____

15. to use _____

16. to turn _____

17. to write _____

18. to seal _____

19. to ride _____

20. to light _____

21. to clean _____

22. to go _____

23. to list _____

24. to color _____

One type of participial phrase is made using the present participle of the verb.

The present participle is formed by adding *ing* to a verb.

Examples: to relax - **relaxing**

to dive - **diving**

to lease - **leasing**

ಹಿಹಿಹಿಹಿಹಿಹಿಹಿಹಿಹಿಹಿಹಿ

Directions: Write the present participle of each verb.

1. to lose   _____

2. to guess   _____

3. to bend   _____

4. to pin   _____

5. to lift   _____

6. to praise   _____

7. to meet   _____

8. to brush   _____

9. to grow   _____

10. to freeze _____

11. to repay   _____

12. to think   _____

13. to push   _____

14. to ask   _____

15. to dust   _____

16. to turn   _____

17. to look   _____

18. to climb   _____

19. to shed   _____

20. to erase   _____

21. to bring   _____

22. to watch _____

23. to deny   _____

24. to sag   _____

Name_____   **Introductory**

Date_____   **Participial Phrases**

A phrase is a group of words. A word standing alone is not a phrase; you must have at least two words.

The present participle is formed by adding *ing* to a verb. A **participial phrase** is formed by using a present participle with another word or words.

　　　　Examples:　　to push - **pushing hard**

　　　　　　　　　　　to smile - **smiling at her brother**

　　　　　　　　　　　to start - **starting the car**

ҙ⧿ҙ⧿ҙ⧿ҙ⧿ҙ⧿ҙ⧿ҙ⧿ҙ⧿ҙ⧿ҙ⧿ҙ

Directions: Write the present participle of the verb. Then, write a participial phrase with it.

　　　Example: to jump - _jumping_ - _jumping on one foot_____

1. to cry - _____ - _____

2. to yell - _____ - _____

3. to reply - _____ - _____

4. to hear - _____ - _____

5. to direct - _____ - _____

6. to move - _____ - _____

7. to pretend - _____ - _____

8. to create - _____ - _____

9. to moisten - _____ - _____

10. to rescue - _____ - _____

Name_____ **Introductory**

Date_____ **Participial Phrases**

A phrase is a group of words. A word standing alone is not a phrase; you must have at least two words.

The present participle is formed by adding *ing* to a verb. A **participial phrase** is formed by using a present participle with another word or words.

Examples: to solve - **solving the puzzle**

to count - **counting by tens**

to annoy - **annoying their sister**

కళ్ళ కళ్ళ కళ్ళ కళ్ళ కళ్ళ కళ్ళ

Directions: Write the present participle of the verb. Then, write a participial phrase with it.

Example: to begin - _beginning_ - _beginning on page one_

1. to live - _____ - _____

2. to hunt - _____ - _____

3. to dab - _____ - _____

4. to bite - _____ - _____

5. to behave - _____ - _____

6. to judge - _____ - _____

7. to agree - _____ - _____

8. to guard - _____ - _____

9. to mutter - _____ - _____

10. to approve - _____ - _____

346

The present participle is formed by adding ***ing*** to a verb. A **participial phrase** is formed by using a present participle with another word or words.

      Example: to decide - deciding to buy a new jacket

Introductory means that the participial phrase begins a sentence. Follow this pattern:

   present participle + word(s) + comma + subject + rest of sentence
      ↕   ↕   ↕   ↕   ↕
   Deciding + to buy a new jacket,   +   Jacob + went to the mall.

Be sure that you end an introductory participial phrase with a **comma** and that

you **place the subject** of the sentence **after the comma**.

                ❧❧❧❧❧❧❧❧❧❧❧

Directions: Write a comma and finish the sentence. Be sure that you place the subject after the comma.

    Example: *Putting up wallpaper,* **Mother climbed on a ladder.**

1. *Stepping onto the ice* _____

   _____

2. *Running down the stairs* _____

   _____

3. *Leaning forward* _____

   _____

4. _Practicing her lines_ _____

    _____

5. _Discovering a hidden cave_ _____

    _____

6. _Waving to the crowd_ _____

    _____

7. _Listening carefully_ _____

    _____

8. _Signing the check_ _____

    _____

9. _Repeating the directions_ _____

    _____

10. _Dropping to his knees_ _____

    _____

11. _Entering the hotel_ _____

    _____

12. _Realizing her mistake_ _____

    _____

The present participle is formed by adding *ing* to a verb. A **participial phrase** is formed by using a present participle with another word or words.

Example: to prepare - <u>preparing for a short vacation</u>

Introductory means that the participial phrase begins a sentence. Follow this pattern:

present participle + word(s) + comma + subject + rest of sentence

Preparing + for a short vacation,   +   Judi + packed a small bag.

Be sure that you end an introductory participial phrase with a **comma** and that

you **place the subject** of the sentence **after the comma**.

ॐॐॐॐॐॐॐॐॐॐॐ

Directions: Write a comma and finish the sentence. Be sure that you place the subject after the comma.

Example: *Laughing loudly,* **she ran off the stage.**

1. *Taking their dog for a walk* _____

_____

2. *Covering her head with a sweater* _____

_____

3. *Looking at pictures in Tom's photo album* _____

_____

4. _Inspecting the back of a ruby ring_

5. _Sipping bottled water_

6. _Making cookies in the shape of Ohio_

7. _Hiding behind a sofa_

8. _Bouncing the basketball_

9. _Recovering from a broken ankle_

10. _Reminding herself to remain calm_

11. _Sliding into home base_

12. _Glancing at his watch_

INDEX